ASPERGER DOWNLOAD

ASPERGER DOWNLOAD

A Guide to Help Teenage Males with Asperger Syndrome Trouble-Shoot Life's Challenges

By Josie & Damian Santomauro

APC

Autism Asperger Publishing Co.
P.O. Box 23173
Shawnee Mission, Kansas 66283-0173
www.asperger.net

©2007 Autism Asperger Publishing Co.
P.O. Box 23173
Shawnee Mission, Kansas 66283-0173
www.asperger.net

Publisher's Cataloging-in-Publication

Santomauro, J. (Josie)

    Asperger download : a guide to help teenage males with Asperger syndrome trouble-shoot life's challenges / by Josie and Damian Santomauro. -- 1st ed. -- Shawnee Mission, Kan. : Autism Asperger Pub. Co., c2007.

    p. ; cm.

    ISBN: 978-1-934575-02-4
    LCCN: 2007933728

    1. Asperger's syndrome in adolescence. 2. Adolescent psychology. 3. Teenage boys--Conduct of life. I. Santomauro, Damian. I. Title. II. Guide to help teenage males with Asperger syndrome.

RJ506.A9 S36 2007
618.92/858832--dc22   0709

This book is designed in and Stone Serif and Gill Sans.

Printed in the United States of America.

*We dedicate this book to all persons with
Asperger Syndrome, from the newly diagnosed
3-year-olds to the recently diagnosed middle-aged.
Without your gifts, unique ways of thinking, and
extraordinary outlook on life, we would have a very stale
and bleak world! Keep up the "aspie-ring" work.*

J & D

FOREWORD

By Dr. Margaret Anne Carter

I have worked with Damian for over 10 years, initially as a school guidance counselor and in more recent years as a behavior change specialist. I am thrilled to write the foreword to this remarkable book.

Damian and Josie provide a marvelous insight into the male teenage world of Asperger Syndrome (AS) – as a teenager with AS and a parent of this teenager. What an extraordinary gift they have created to male teenagers with AS and to those of us who "walk with" them. I categorize myself in the latter group, and thank both of them for venturing into the unfamiliar terrain of child-parent dialogue, describing life events from very different, yet in some ways rather similar, perspectives.

Josie's and Damian's relationship is rather exceptional. Through their dialogue, the reader gets a sense that Josie plays the role of Damian's problem "helper" rather than his problem solver. Her responses give us insight into how she has guided and supported Damian through his teenage years, purposely avoiding doing for him what he has the skills and competencies to accomplish on his own. The real key to Damian's and Josie's relationship is Josie loving, valuing, appreciating, accepting and respecting Damian for himself, for who he is.

The dialogue between Damian and Josie is intriguing, with Damian providing advice and knowledge based on his personal real-life experiences. Josie's responses as a parent are worthy of note – sometimes affirming, at other times supporting, always respectful. Josie's perspective reveals her in the roles of caring nurturer, coaching teacher, astute manager and wise leader.

Asperger Download gives the reader the opportunity to learn more about the way Damian thinks and processes life experiences. As such, this book is beneficial on many fronts – in gaining more appreciation and depth of understanding of how male teenagers with AS may perceive and think about the social world; how influential parents can be with their teenagers; and how "help from special teachers and personal determination" (Damian's wording) make a significant difference in the life of individuals.

I like the way each topic is clearly defined before the dialogue begins. This gives the reader the same definition of a given topic as the writers. No mystery or guesswork involved.

The range of topics is broad, with Damian and Josie covering the unsavory, solemn, tough, as well as the pleasant and pleasurable sides of teenage living. This is what makes this book so "real" – it embraces themes that "cross the divide." The reader is invited on a fascinating journey, learning how to deal with life's ups and downs from Damian's and Josie's perspectives.

As I read *Asperger Download*, I have the impression that Damian's down-to-earth explanations and advice are intertwined with a complex web of interlocking emotions and thoughts about himself and how he sees and is seen by others. Damian conveys a mixture of emotions – sometimes humor, at other times joy, frustration, confusion, surprise, discomfort, amusement and happiness. This is what adds value to the book – a sense of the personal in a social world that can be both mystifying, yet very straightforward. An oxymoron indeed!

Asperger Download is an excellent addition to your teenage son's bookshelf.

– Margaret Carter, Ph.D.
   Author, consultant and therapist

INTRODUCTION

★ My son, Damian, was diagnosed with Asperger Syndrome (AS) at the age of 5. He is now 17, and after 12 years of intervention is doing very well and has just ventured out into his first year of university/college. He claims to have "combated" AS (his words). By this I am guessing he means that he copes well in society with the skills and strategies he has learned along the way. He said he'd like to talk about how he has coped with AS, so I asked him if he would like to share his "wisdom" in an A-to-Z book for teens with AS. And, as you can see, he took me up on it.

This resource targets the 11- to-17-year-old age range, and is intended as a basic A-to-Z teaching tool for teens with AS, touching on general life and social situations they may come across. It is written specifically for teens with AS from the point of view of a teen with AS – his experiences and his advice. My comments, which follow Damian's, will be more prescriptive and constructive, just touching on Damian's work. My comments may help those who care for teens with AS gain further understanding.

The topics were chosen because they represent life, challenges and all the social rules – spoken or not – that teens with AS may encounter. The reader can either choose to read from A to Z in order at his leisure, flip open to any topic, or be guided by the categories listed in the back of the book. Topics can also be used for immediate assistance/guidance for a certain challenge that has arisen. Be guided by your teen's maturity. Is he able to read this on his own? Or does he require the guidance of an adult? You could even choose a topic each day and discuss this as a family or at school in a small group.

At first Damian presumed he just had to explain what each topic meant. My challenge was to help him understand that he was to share his personal experiences. We had a slight communication problem; we needed a bridge to relay the message. I found two bridges. One was an adult with AS (thanks, Rob!), who explained to Damian what I had been trying to say, but in a different way – an Aspie way. The other bridge was when I asked Damian to imagine that he was trying to explain the topics to a friend of his who has AS with high needs. The light bulb went on, and Damian modified his topics by adding his personal experiences.

As I went through Damian's contributions, I was impressed with his insight and wisdom and am honored to collaborate on this project with him. Although at times it seemed to be a long and drawn-out process, we made it through. I am confident this resource will benefit not only young adult males with Asperger Syndrome gain confidence in themselves and their day-to-day activities, but also bring relief to their parents, teachers and others, knowing that there is now a resource that touches on crucial but also sensitive topics. • Josie

My name is Damian and I was diagnosed with Asperger Syndrome when I was 5. I have just graduated from high school and am attending university this year to study science. Asperger Syndrome, though it is being defined as a disability, has benefited me greatly in my life. It has made me think logically and helped me through my studies. But at the same time, having Asperger Syndrome also means that I lacked the social skills to get along successfully in society. At times, it was very stressful not being like other people my age and feeling like an outcast because I couldn't interact with them socially. With help from special teachers and personal determination, I have learned acceptable social skills. I wish that back then the topics in this book had been explained to me, but unfortunately I had to learn from experience. I hope that this book will benefit all young aspies and make the social learning process a little easier for them. • Damian

ABUSE – To insult, exploit, ill-treat or hurt someone badly

Abuse is basically something upsetting. There is verbal abuse (insults and putdowns), emotional abuse (harassment, etc.) and physical abuse (fighting and beating someone up). If you are being abused, seek help, either from a friend or a teacher. Abuse can lead to long-term psychological damage, which is a bad thing. I've been verbally abused many times, and I didn't handle it very well. I used to get into fights and stuff like bashing people. I regret doing that now. I wish I knew then how to handle it better; hopefully you'll take my advice and not become violent. • Damian

Because you are different from other teenagers in some respects, you may be the victim of abuse from people who don't understand you or your behaviors. Damian's comment about wishing he knew how to handle it better is very important. You have many choices of how to handle these types of situations – talk to an adult about what your best choices would be. • Josie

ACNE – Lots of inflamed pimples on face, back or chest

Acne is a condition where you have pimples on your face. Usually you have to have a lot of pimples for it to be called acne. This can be caused by stress and unexpressed anger that builds up. If you get acne, you can do two things. First, try and stop the anger and stress in your life, or at least try to express it in a nonviolent way. The second thing is to use pimple cream. Don't rub or scratch; this can leave scars and only aggravate the condition. • Damian

★ Acne can also be a result of hormonal imbalances or be related to diet; for example, high-sugar diets. Perhaps you should go see a doctor and get it checked out. If acne medication is recommended, do some research on what types would suit you, as some medications can heal the acne but have other negative side effects. • Josie

ADOLESCENCE – Teenage, youth – the time between puberty and maturity

Adolescence means the teen years. For some people this is the best part of life! So try to enjoy it while you can. If you're not enjoying it for any reason (maybe because of immature bullying or maybe because you feel that you don't get a fair say in your own life), don't think that the rest of your life is going to be worse. Some people who hated adolescence love adulthood. Me? I love adolescence. I get scared of aging too quickly, because I know my adolescence is probably going to be the most fun time of my life. There were times when I wasn't enjoying it, getting depressed and stuff, but I knew that if I waited, I would eventually get happier. • Damian

★ Damian is right. You have your ups and downs in your adolescent years. It may be a little harder for you because you feel that you are different than other teens. Just go with the flow; take each day and moment as it comes and learn from each experience, whether it's positive or negative. Remember, nothing ever stays the same! • Josie

ADULTHOOD – Mature and grown up

Adulthood is the stage in life after being a teenager (adolescence). Adults have more authority over teenagers, so we have to listen to what they have to say (darn!). • Damian

★ Gee, Damian, we can't force you to listen to us adults, but it would be nice if you did listen sometimes! Besides, many children and teens with AS actually prefer the company of adults to people their own age. I think that might be because you are quite intelligent and a bit more mature than your peer group. • Josie

ADVICE – Suggestion, recommendation or opinion on what to do about a situation

Advice is a statement that is said to help you with a situation, like if I like a girl and my friend suggests that I ask her out. If someone gives you advice, don't get angry with him or her just because you don't like the advice. Be grateful he or she cares enough for you to be willing to give you advice. Then choose what you want to do. If you can, I suggest you take or at least consider all advice given to you. People who give you advice are usually in a neutral position. People in a neutral position always have a better view of the situation, like a spectator in a computer game who can see what all players are doing, not just one. The problem is that sometimes people give you lots of different advice. Whenever this happens, I just listen to all of them and repeat what they said in my head. Whichever feels best I choose. • Damian

★ Wise young man, Damian! Yes, if you are confused about something, sometimes you can ask others for advice – somebody you trust. A good thing to do is as Damian says, listen to all the advice and work out what's best for you. It is even better if you can listen to your own advice. Ask yourself what advice you would give somebody who was in the same position as you. • Josie

ALCOHOL – Colorless intoxicating liquid

Being drunk isn't a good thing. In fact, in many countries, including the United States, it is illegal and can have serious consequences if you drink alcohol under the legal age (each state and country has differing legal ages). Nevertheless, some people try to get drunk due to peer pressure, and others get drunk to try and forget something they don't like. Some just get drunk because they have had too much to drink without knowing it. Don't drink! Besides being against the law in many places, drinking can make you do stupid things because it impairs your judgment. Also, you can get sick to your stomach, etc. • Damian

The good news is that Damian has realized that alcohol isn't such a great thing and is telling his friends that they all drink too much and should try to have fun without drinking ... yay! What I think happened with Damian and alcohol is that the first time he truly experienced it, he only had a little, but he had fun (it wasn't over the top, too much). But then he wanted to experience this feeling again and again, so he became a bit obsessed with alcohol and just didn't know what his limit was. This is why he binge drank: to try to get that feeling quicker. But he didn't realize that binge drinking is dangerous because you can get alcohol poisoning from it. It also affects your liver, and you aren't really fully in control of what you are saying or doing. It's not a very safe position to be in. • Josie

ANGER – Strong feelings of rage and fury

Anger is extremely negative. It's when you dislike someone or hate someone or something. It's a bit hard to explain what it is. It's okay to get angry, because if you don't express it, it will build up and then explode! One of the ways I express anger is by swearing. Not excessively, because then it becomes inappropriate. Some people don't like that way of expressing themselves, but it works for me. It releases my anger in small quantities. It's better to swear than to go out and physically express your anger. But in some situations (like maybe at school or other places) and in some households, swearing isn't allowed. If this is the case for you, it can help to write about what's making you angry or talk about it to people. You can even do stuff such as go for a swim. There are many ways to express your anger in nonviolent ways. I believe that anger is a product of fear. Whenever you get angry, it may be because you are afraid of something. Like if someone insults you and you get angry, maybe it's because you are afraid that what they said is true. If you don't get angry in a situation like that, you obviously know that what they're saying isn't true and getting angry over it won't solve anything. • Damian

All teenagers experience anger; it's okay to express it, so long as you release your anger appropriately. I recently purchased Damian a punching bag. This is another great way to express anger … and I joked about putting my photo on it so when he was angry with me he could go and punch the bag! Also, as Damian said, writing about it is a good way to express anger. Damian actually writes lots of poetry about things that make him angry and frustrated. We have included some of his poetry near the end of this book. There are many degrees of anger, from low-grade to severe anger. Most of the time anger is about not having control over a situation. There are strategies other than the punching bag that you can use if you can feel anger begin to build up inside of you, such as controlled breathing and meditation. Sometimes if you have high anxiety, this can cross over the line into an anger outburst, because you are so anxious, stressed and on edge that just one little thing can set you off – just like the full glass of water, just one extra drop of water added can spill the water over. • Josie

ANXIETY – When you feel worried, nervous, agitated, scared or tense

Anxiety is like stress or worry. I used to get very anxious and get panic attacks and stuff from the smallest things. Like, for example, I'd leave home to go to school and I'd be on the bus and then, "OH CRAP! Did I lock the door??" The biggest shock would come over me, and I'd get so stressed I'd bite my knuckles until they were red. I'd worry about it all day until I came home, only to find out I did lock the door. For this specific example, I just make sure that now when I lock the door, I'm concentrating on locking the door, instead of being in autopilot mode and thinking about other stuff while I'm instinctively locking it. For other things, like thinking I've forgotten something, I just think that I probably didn't forget it and I use logic to realize that it's too late to go back and get it and there's no benefit from stressing over it. • Damian

Yes, Damian's panic attacks were not fun. Anxiety may be one of the challenges you have with AS. If you are highly anxious all the time, it's probably a good thing to talk to somebody about it and learn some strategies for calming your anxieties. I used to be an anxious person in my younger years; now I say to myself, "What's the worse thing that can happen?" and that usually helps put it into perspective. Slowing down to problem solve and learning some breathing techniques are also good strategies. • Josie

APOLOGY – A plea for forgiveness, acknowledging fault and regret

Apologies are basically saying you are sorry for something you did. If someone apologizes to you, it's good manners to accept. If you apologize to someone, that doesn't lower your position; it makes you a better person. Also, if you apologize and the other person accepts, all conflict and unnecessary anger (see Anger) can be erased. • Damian

Yes, good point, Damian. It's a very hard thing to apologize, so if someone does apologize to you, acknowledge it by saying "thank you." Saying "thank you" doesn't always mean you have forgotten or forgiven, but it does show the other person that you appreciate his or her apology. If you need to apologize for something you have done and are finding it hard to do, just put yourself in the position of the other person and see his side of the situation. Maybe you will then find it easier to apologize. If you are stubborn and won't apologize, that might be your pride holding you back. Remember, apologizing doesn't mean you have done something wrong; sometimes we apologize for how we said something that was interpreted differently from what we intended. For example, sometimes if I have had a disagreement with a friend, I will say, "I'm sorry that we had this disagreement. I would still like to be your friend." But just because I apologized doesn't mean I was saying I was wrong and my friend was right. • Josie

ARGUMENTS – Discussions where there are disputes, debates or disagreements

An argument is like a verbal fight. It's similar to a debate, only there is no order; and an argument, unlike a debate, is often overrun with anger. There is usually no neutral person to see which side is right (if any side), and because no one is willing to back down, it goes on and on and on. If you get into an argument, you could just say "whatever" and walk away. There aren't many things that can be said against that. I've started to say "whatever" and it works. • Damian

Damian and I have arguments sometimes. When he tries the "whatever" with me, I usually say, ''Don't you 'whatever' me!'' It's okay to disagree with somebody else's point of view; if we all thought the same, the world would be a boring place. But sometimes we get caught up in trying to convince the other person that our point of view is the right one and theirs is wrong. In many situations, it is best just to agree to disagree and get on with life. • Josie

ASPERGER SYNDROME – A pervasive development disorder related to autism

Asperger Syndrome is an autism spectrum disorder (ASD) that I have and that supposedly one in every 150 people has (the number is increasing). It used to be a big deal when I was diagnosed. When I was first diagnosed, we were told that there was only 1 in 10,000 people who had ASD. Now it's a lot better and easier to get help. There are a lot more resources and services for people with ASD. • Damian

Yes, I remember when Damian was first diagnosed with AS. I didn't know what it was. So I thought the worst – that it was a degenerative disease and that he was going to die from it. The only information we were given was a paper that a university student had written on the topic. Like Damian said, nowadays there are so many resources available. I have always encouraged Damian to learn about AS so he has a clear understanding of his needs and challenges, but also never to blame his AS for behaviors he could control and to look at the positives that having AS brings to his life. When mothers of newly diagnosed children call me and they are feeling sad, I say, "Welcome to the wonderful world of Asperger Syndrome." There are many positives to having AS, such as brilliance in the world of science, intelligence and special talents of many kinds. • Josie

BELIEVING IN YOURSELF – Accepting yourself and all things about you

Always believe in yourself and that you can do whatever you put your mind to. I know this sounds like a corny line that adults like to use, but it is true. Where there's a will, there's a way. And remember, you are always going to be better than you think you are. There were so many times in my life when I didn't believe in myself, but now I look back and think, "Why didn't I?" and I regret not doing something because I know I could have done it. Maybe I could have been Student Council president if I applied, if I believed that I could win the election. But because I didn't believe in myself, I will never know. • Damian

★ Good points, Damian. You don't want to go through life regretting not trying something because you didn't believe you could. Remember, "believing you can't do something" is just your mind tricking you. It's just a thought. So if you create a thought that says, "you can't do it," then you can also create a thought that says, "you **can** do it." If you have low self-esteem, you most probably have an underlying lack of belief in yourself. The key here is to tackle skill building and problem solving. Self-esteem will follow. • Josie

BITING – Piercing or chewing something with your teeth

Biting is like trying to eat someone. I don't suggest you bite someone. If you bite someone, usually people will think of you as weird, and it could un-necessarily hurt the person you're biting. Also, what if they have some kind of skin disease or something? If you bite them, have a guess where some of that disease may go? In your mouth, down your throat, into your system and then into your skin. I used to bite myself because I was frustrated and stressed. Sometimes I still bite my knuckles, but only when I'm massively worried about something. • Damian

★ Hmm, I think Damian is exaggerating about getting a skin disease. Don't panic! Biting is usually an extreme behavior that comes from stress or feeling there's no way out – a form of communicating your anger or frustra-tion. It would be good if you could learn strategies for how to calm yourself before you get to the biting stage. If you feel you are at the biting stage, stop

whatever is happening, try to take a deep breath, think about something else you can do that is not harmful to yourself or anybody around you; take some time out. • Josie

BODY SHAPE – The appearance of your physical structure

 Some people get paranoid about their body shape and appearance. This is usually because they want to attract people of the opposite sex. Many go on diets and stuff, but that often doesn't work, either because the diet isn't that great or because the diet isn't followed properly. Some people get really paranoid about their weight and how much they eat. This can become a serious problem and can lead to eating disorders such as anorexia and bulimia. I used to have anorexia because I thought I was fat. I only ate a small dinner all day, and I did 100 push-ups and 100 sit-ups every night. It was not good for me, and I was getting pale and really skinny. I finally came to realize that I could have a good body and not worry about what I eat. Now I eat almost whatever I want, but I still exercise. • Damian

Everyone's body shape is different, and we shouldn't compare ourselves to models in magazines or other people. Who made the rules of what a body should look like? Don't be influenced by television or magazines about what a body should or shouldn't look like. The important thing is to be healthy and fit. Yes, there was a stage when Damian became obsessed with body image and had an eating disorder. He did not eat all day and only ate a small dinner. He lost too much weight and ended up being sick and refused to see that he was out of control until I took him to a doctor. • Josie

BULLYING – To hurt, frighten, push around and dominate a person

Bullying is a common activity at some schools whereby, in my experience, some of the "Jocks" (see Jocks) and the "socially great" like to perform on people who are different from them. It can be expressed in a variety of forms, which include name-calling, violence and sometimes just exclusion. If someone tries to bully you, you have several options for stopping it from happening or affecting you. One of those choices is to just ignore it. Bullies bully to get a reaction, which amuses and entertains them. It also makes them feel better than you. If you ignore them, their entertainment goes away, and they can't feel better about themselves because they failed at creating a reaction. Another choice is to report the bullying to a teacher or other adult. I know that some teenagers say, "Solve your own problems! Don't go to a teacher!" and stuff like that, but in some cases, it is the right thing to do. A third option is to create a good comeback (see Comebacks), one that is smart and witty and can't backfire. Don't create stupid comebacks, which will leave you open to more insults. If you can't think of a good comeback, just look at the bully and smirk as if you find his insult so petty that it's funny. Another option, which will not help you at all, is to use violence (see Violence). This will only result in both of you getting hurt and you getting into trouble. If that ends up happening, the bully wins! • Damian

I agree with Damian's view of bullying. The dictionary says that a bully is "a noisy, overbearing person who tyrannizes over the weak; he domineers, intimidates, overawes, ill treats." We imagine the bully as a bit of a monster, but bullies come in all shapes and sizes. Your bus driver, sister, swim coach or even your grandmother could be a bully in disguise. Bullies come in all shapes, sizes, ages, etc. You do not need to be suspicious of everybody, though. If you are being bullied, act on it, and report it to a friend, teacher or other adult.

Bullies are only looking at feeding their power. Bullying comes in all forms of abuse and can happen at school, outside school, at work, in your neighborhood, through your mobile phone or on the Internet; for example, a chat room. In fact, this is becoming more and more common.

The victim needs help to learn coping strategies and also to understand why he may attract bullies. Victims may have negative beliefs about themselves and low self-esteem that are making them easy targets to be bullied, or they appear "different" in some way. Don't feel like a victim, and you you are less likely to be bullied! • Josie

CAREER – A profession or occupation that you train for or work in

A career is basically a job. But instead of being stuck in the same position forever, as you might if you didn't pursue a career, you get promotions and move up the ladder as you gain experience, take special training, and so on. If you're looking into a career, I suggest you choose a career you enjoy. My mom's advice to me about getting a career was to get one I enjoyed, but my dad's advice was to get one with high pay, because there's no point in getting a career that you like and get lousy pay.

This was very confusing and extremely contradictory. So I came up with my own advice: Get your favorite career with high pay! I like the career I'm getting into. I've got a traineeship at a laboratory, which is really cool, because I want to be a scientist when I get into the workforce. If you like something and you want a career in something you like, then look into a traineeship or apprenticeship at your school. • Damian

Yes, Damian has made the preliminary steps to take him to his career. If you are confused about what you want to do, it can help to remember back to when you were little and what you wanted to be when you "grew up." Since Damian was a little boy, he wanted to be a scientist. When he was 8 years old, he had a laboratory under the staircase at our home where he had a microscope, took things apart, and so on. And when I was a little girl, I always wanted to be an author. I did other jobs when I was an adult and was never really happy until I was 35 and thought, "Yes, I still want to be an author," so I became one! To help in your search, think of your special interests and talents; they often lead the way to your career path. • Josie

CHAT ROOMS – Places on the Internet where you "talk" to other people

Chat rooms are web sites or online programs with a chat box where people can chat socially. They are like instant messages sent between people. Chat rooms essentially allow people to talk online without paying for a telephone call, which is pretty good! If someone starts harassing you in a chat rooms, block that person if you can, or close the chat site and don't go back to it. Some chat programs have an option to save your conversations, so if the harassment was so bad that you want evidence of it, save your conversation. If you can't find a save option, print a screenshot. To print a screenshot for Windows users press Ctrl + Prt Sc, then open paint (or any picture-editing software) and press Ctrl + v. I'm not sure what it is for other operating systems, but it's probably something similar. • Damian

Chat rooms can be both good and bad. Good because you can experience social talk online with friends, but bad because sometimes you don't know with whom you are chatting. Don't believe everything you see or read online. If the person you are chatting to says he is a 10-year-old boy, he could really be a 54-year-old man in disguise. Do not give anybody your personal information over the Internet, like where you live or what your phone number is. The safest chat online is instant messaging, where you have control over whom you chat with and whom you invite to chat with you. If you are being harassed in a chat room, report it to the moderator. • Josie

COMEBACK – A clever or amusing answer

A comeback is a response to an insult, usually from a bully (see Bully). It is important to create a good comeback, otherwise people will just tease. Try to brainstorm for a second, but stop before you blurt out the comeback you came up with. If using a comeback will get you into a lot of trouble, like maybe the person you're using the comeback on is some huge bulky monster or your teacher, DON'T DO IT! Making a comeback isn't that important, so if you can't think of a good one, you're better off not giving one.

On a ski trip at my school there was this guy who was trying to insult me in front of everyone. I can't remember what he was saying, but I responded, "At least I don't have man boobs!" and everyone burst out laughing. I know it was a mean thing to say but, seriously, if someone is starting it, they're asking for it! Remember that. • Damian

Hmm, "man boobs." Yes funny, but a bit nasty, Damian! I think the wisest thing to do is say nothing or walk away. I know it can be hard to do because you can feel the anger building up and you want to lash out, but by walking away you are taking your self-power with you and not giving it away by responding. • Josie

COMMUNICATION – Transmitting and receiving information or signals

Communication is important in nearly everything. In math, communication is important; otherwise, people just see a bunch of random numbers. In English, it's obviously important. In life it's important. An example of communication is talking with someone to arrange something, or talking with someone to inform him or her of something. It's a little hard to explain what it is, but you get the idea. Another way of saying it: It's understanding each other in talking, writing, typing, and so on. Due to our AS, we sometimes find it harder to communicate. Just talking, I only hear about two-thirds of a sentence and I'll be like "What? Say again?" I have to try to listen more carefully. • Damian

Damian is right; one of the challenges of AS is in the area of communication. It is important that people working with you, such as teachers, understand that you may have difficulty with communication so they can help out. Because communication works two ways, it's a good idea if you also try to help yourself out. As Damian said, he tries to listen more carefully. Another idea is that if you have a teacher who does a lot of talking to the class, ask for notes to take away and study or get permission to voice record the class and play it back later on your own. • Josie

CONFIDENCE – A feeling of trust and fearlessness within yourself

(Also see Believe in Yourself) Confidence is important in life. You must feel good about yourself in order to be happy. And why wouldn't you feel good about yourself? If people say bad things about you and comment about things you can't do, they are ignorant and should not be listened to. You can do anything if you want to. If you want to do something, DO IT! Unless, of course, it results in someone getting hurt or something, like if you're angry. Then don't do it. Do positive things to help people. Trust me; you will feel a lot better if you do that than if you hurt someone. Also, if you have a girl in mind that you like, remember that girls like people who are confident. • Damian

Confidence is based on your self-esteem. If you feel good about yourself, then you are a confident person. I think Damian covered the topic nicely. • Josie

CONFUSION – A mix of random things that create a state of disorder

Confusion is basically mayhem in the brain. You are not sure what's happening, and in some extreme cases of confusion you don't have a clue about what is happening. Confusion usually is the result of lack of instructions or lack of information. If you're confused about something, it's not your fault, unless you purposely weren't listening to whoever was instructing you. If you innocently didn't hear or weren't informed about something, then ask. If someone teases you about your confusion, that person is obviously a cold-hearted person who is quite ignorant and jumps to conclusions.

I remember once at school we had to do a project on complex numbers. I was confused because I had been away when they showed the video to explain it, and every time I asked the teacher, she said I "should have known" and didn't explain to me what the project was about. So I got information from other students and thought I knew what I was doing. I did the project, handed it in and got a D, the lowest grade in the class. I was like "WHAT??" I was even more confused, because I did exactly what all the other students had done. I hate that the teacher never properly explained it. In the future, I will be more persistent about asking for clarification. • Damian

As Damian wrote, this is an example of when it's very important that teachers and your school are aware of your AS-related challenges. Confusion occurs because communication is lacking or is poor and you don't have all the information that you need. A way to find your way out of confusion is to ask for help; ask questions or research the topic. • Josie

COOL – Fashionable, modern and "with-it" in attitude and style of dress

Cool? Um … well, what can I say? Socially, it means good. It's not necessary to be "cool." Don't let others intimidate you by saying that what you do isn't cool because it doesn't matter what others think; only what you think. If you try to be "cool" and you become something other than who you are, it isn't a good thing. I tried it once, and at first I thought I knew who I was; it actually took about six months before I questioned who I was and that process wasn't nice. I tried to be tough because that was what was "cool" at the time, but it required too much of an aggressive attitude. So save the time, and do what you like instead of what others like. • Damian

Yes, I remember that time when Damian tried to be "cool." He imitated the cool people that he admired. He never liked jeans, hated the way they felt on his legs. Then all of a sudden, because he noticed that it was cool to wear jeans, he wanted jeans and got three pairs. To go with the jeans, he wanted a polo shirt (t-shirt with a collar) because this is what all the cool guys were wearing. Unfortunately, because of his obsessive behaviors, he ended up with 30 of these polo shirts, he just didn't know when to stop buying them. Trying to be "cool" didn't work well for Damian, because it didn't come naturally to him. I just kept saying to him, "be who you really are, not what others are." You might like somebody's style and want to be similar; that's okay, but when trying to change yourself becomes stressful (as it was for Damian), then it's not the right thing to do. I think it's about wanting to be accepted. You want to be accepted by everyone and you see the "cool" people being popular and being accepted, so you try to copy them. Just be natural; don't try too hard and accept yourself for who you are, then others are more likely to accept you too. You cannot expect everybody to like you, but the ones who do will be your true friends, and that's the most important thing. • Josie

COUNSELOR – A person who advises, guides, recommends and instructs

A counselor is someone who you can talk to about things you are worried about or not sure of. If your parent suggests that you see a counselor, then I recommend you do so. It is extremely helpful, even if you don't think you need help. I still see a counselor, and she helped me through a lot. Sometimes even when you are finished with one counselor, after a long time you might need to see another because other problems arise. I've seen three different counselors, and each one has helped me a lot. • Damian

A counselor is a neutral person you can talk to about your problems or fears. Counselors don't judge you or dislike you or bring any negative feelings into the session. A counselor is basically there to listen and offer guidance. Then it's up to you what you choose to do with the advice; you always have the power and choice to do what you want. There are many counselors who specialize in and understand AS. • Josie

CRIME – An illegal act

Crime is BAD! It's basically breaking the law. If you get caught doing something really bad, you might screw up your future. Don't do anything that you feel uneasy about. If your friends or others try to pressure you into doing something like this, don't do it, because the consequence is probably not worth the adventure. I've been very, very tempted to do illegal things, but I know that I have a huge future ahead of me and what I would get out of the illegal act is not worth ruining my future, so I haven't done anything like that. • Damian

Well, since Damian wrote that statement, he HAS been in trouble with the law. He purchased alcohol for his friends, even though he was under the legal age. He didn't think it would be such a big deal and definitely didn't think he would get caught. Police approached him straightaway, and then he lied to them about his name! He didn't think that was against the law. He thought they would go away to check it, but they checked while he waited and then took him down to the police station. He was given a warning because he hadn't been in trouble with the law before. But in your area the law may be much stricter than our local police were, so don't take a chance. I think Damian has learned from this, as having a criminal record can ruin some career choices and even traveling overseas. Now Damian is telling his friends not to commit any crimes. A lot of teenagers with AS can become innocently caught in a criminal act, so be extra careful. I think Damian wanted to be a bit of a hero (sorry Damian!) in front of his friends, so he offered to buy the alcohol because he thought he looked the oldest. • Josie

D

DAD – Your father or stepfather

 Your dad is your male parent. It is important to have a balanced relationship between both of your parents to have a healthy childhood. Seeing your dad often and doing activities with him is important, if possible, especially for guys, because guys use their dad as a father figure, and they need that father figure to relate to. • Damian

I agree with Damian that it's important to have a male role model, especially if you are male yourself. If you don't have a father or stepfather, then maybe a grandparent, uncle or a good family friend can be your male role model. Your father plays equally as important a role as your mother. Your male role model may provide you with skills such as leadership and self-confidence. Also, males often "bond" over certain activities and hobbies they share.• Josie

DATING – A social engagement with somebody, usually of the opposite gender

Dating is when you go somewhere with someone of the opposite sex (example, boyfriend or girlfriend), or in some cases with somebody of the same sex. If you go on your first date, don't worry too much and don't try to put on an act, just be yourself and be confident about yourself (see Confidence). If you feel that you should hold hands, then do so; if your date rejects you (which is unlikely when it comes to holding hands), then don't be embarrassed, just think that he/she isn't the right person for you or that you acted too quickly. The same goes when it comes to kissing (see Kissing), but unfortunately there's a higher chance for rejection with kissing. Kissing on the first date is a bit weird; I know some girls at my school who got pissed off at their dates for not kissing on the first date, while other girls don't like kissing on the first date. Do what you feel is best because it probably is the best choice.

Now for who pays for the date expenses: It used to be the guy who paid, but it SHOULD now be whoever asks. I once went on a date with a girl, and I spent so much money on the date even though she asked me, and then she dumped me … the next day! I wasn't worried about losing her; I was worried about the MONEY! Don't make the same mistake; the person who asks should pay. Try to find fun stuff to do on a date. I went to the movies on my first date. Be creative, and try to find out what the other person likes too. • Damian

Damian has covered most of this topic. The paying bit can be a bit confusing, so you might ask the opinion of your parents or your friends. A lot of dates nowadays are "Dutch." This means you go halves in any expenses. • Josie

DECISIONS – To make up your mind about choices

Decisions, decisions … Throughout your whole life, you'll be making lots of decisions. You've made a decision by deciding to read this book, this letter (the letter D), and even this word (Decisions). But these decisions aren't that important in comparison to some of the decisions you'll have to make in the future, such as your school subjects, your university, post-graduate courses, and your career. You'll be making personal decisions such as whether to get married or not, whether to have children or not, and so on. If there is a decision that you can't make for yourself, ask for some advice (see Advice). Advice is always helpful when making major decisions. To make a sound decision, go get all pros and cons regarding the situation. When you do that, you can usually see which decision is the best. When I had to decide which university to go to, I added up the pros and cons for each university. After seeking advice and researching the best courses for me, I easily came to a decision. • Damian

⭐ Yes, great advice regarding the pros and cons, Damian. If you are finding it hard to make a decision and become more confused the more you think about it, make up a list with two columns, PROS & CONS. Then fill out the columns for each choice and sit back and look at the list and base your decision on it. • Josie

DEPRESSION – Feeling sad, gloomy and miserable for a long time

Depression is when you're really, really sad. Depression is quite common. I suffered from depression even before I knew what depression meant. I had it for a long time, and I still sometimes get depressed. If you get depressed, try to find out why. It is always good to ask for help or at least tell someone. Maybe even talk to them about the reason you are depressed, if you know of a reason. Your parents/guardians are always a good option. You should know that you're never alone with your concerns. • Damian

⭐ Since writing that, Damian once again fell into a deep depression. His symptoms were feeling sad, feeling tired and exhausted, feeling anxious; his grades dropped, and he didn't enjoy hobbies or interests that he usually

liked to do. Depression can be caused by mental or physical reasons and is pretty common among adolescents with AS. At first I thought that Damian might have been depressed because of the incident he had with the police as his depression happened soon after this, that he felt saddened and ashamed about the whole thing. But after some blood tests, his doctor discovered that it was due to physical reasons. Talk to an adult about how you are feeling and go see your doctor if your depressed mood continues; it's not nice OR healthy to feel that way all the time. • Josie

DIAGNOSIS – Analysis, investigation or prognosis

I remember when I was first being diagnosed. I was in a little room with a lady and there was a mirrored wall next to me. I wondered why the mirror was there. When I looked closer, I realized that I could see through it. I saw my mom and dad and some other adults. I remember waving at them every 5 minutes instead of listening to what the lady was saying to me. I was 5 years old then, and I wasn't told I had AS until I was 9! I believe that being told that you are diagnosed is important because it creates more understanding about yourself. • Damian

Damian was diagnosed 12 years ago by a diagnostic team consisting of a pediatrician, a speech therapist, an occupational therapist and a psychiatrist. They each performed various tests and as a team came up with the diagnosis of Asperger Syndrome. When Damian was diagnosed in 1994, there wasn't much information available about AS. I thought he was too young to be given that big piece of information verbally. I waited until he would ask me, and at age 9 he started to ask questions like, "Why aren't I like other boys? Why do I have a teacher aide?" That's when I knew that I had to tell him about his diagnosis. But it is different in each case. It is a family decision. Being a writer, I decided to write a booklet for him called **The Mystery of a Special Kid** and read it to him. Since then, he has had his ups and downs with his diagnosis; there have been times when Damian said he didn't "have" Asperger or that he was "cured." But the older he gets, the more accepting he has become as

he is involved in his own management and health. Damian even speaks at conferences to teachers about being a student with AS. So nowadays he is more comfortable with his diagnosis. • Josie

DIET – What one eats and drinks

Diet can really affect my behavior! If I eat too much wheat or dairy, I become moody, cranky and mischievous. (Or at least that's what I've been told). I personally can't always tell that my behavior changes, but my family can. I no longer eat lots of wheat or dairy, and I drink goat's or soymilk instead of cow's milk. You might think "Goat's milk? Ewwww! That's disgusting!" But I love it. The first time I tried it, I loved it. When I do try normal milk now, I think it tastes like water. Soymilk I used to hate. Mom tried to introduce it to me when I was 10. I never liked it until about a few years ago, and I love it now. I eat wheat-free food, such as gluten-free bread, gluten-free pasta, basically anything gluten-free. • Damian

A lot of people with AS have what is called Leaky Gut Syndrome. Basically, it means that you have some food intolerance that affects the way your stomach absorbs food and releases toxins into your nervous system, and in turn affects your behavior and learning. If you want to learn more about it, do some research. With Damian, we found that once his diet changed, his behavior and clarity of mind improved. • Josie

DISABILITY – An inability to achieve a certain capacity or function

A disability is the opposite of ability. It makes you not able to do something, like a broken back may make it impossible for someone to walk. That is an example of a physical disability. There are other disabilities, such as ADD and AS. Mental disabilities are different than physical; for one thing, they affect the brain, not the body (unless the part of the brain that it affects is a part that controls the body). "Disability" is a bit of a touchy word, especially with someone who has a non-physical disability that is not visible. Like us! We have a non-physical disability. When people ask me what AS is, I have a little difficulty explaining it. When I was first told I had AS, I didn't understand it very well, which made it even more difficult to tell someone else about it. • Damian

The word "disability" seems like a negative word, but it doesn't have to be. You can turn it around and say you have an "ability" and take note of all the special gifts you have because of your AS. For example, Damian is very gifted in math and science, which seems to be a classic characteristic of AS. Because of his ability to study intensely, he will go on to become a good scientist and possibly find the cure for cancer … all because he has AS! • Josie

DIVORCE – To officially end a marriage or union

A divorce is a permanent breakup between two people who are married. A divorce is never about the kids, but about the couple. If your parents get a divorce, don't think it has anything to do with you, because how could it? Also, never get angry with them for getting a divorce. A divorce happens because your parents lose feelings for each other; how would you feel if you had to live in the same house with someone you didn't like any more? When my parents got divorced, I didn't care too much. I just remember sitting on my bed and thinking that things would change, because they always do. I live with my mom but see my dad every week, and the time I spend with him now is better than the time we used to spend together, because it's more special since it's only once a week. So that might even mean that for me it was a good thing for my parents to have gotten a divorce since I'm now closer to my dad. • Damian

★ I remember when Damian's dad and I got divorced. It didn't seem to affect Damian as much as it did his sister. She was very upset. Damian didn't turn it into an emotional event; he just saw the logical side of it all. Other people with AS may have reacted differently. • Josie

DOCTOR – A medical practitioner whose intention is to heal a patient

 There are doctors other than the ones you go to for a cold. Sometimes you will see special doctors for certain things. For example, if your vision is blurred, you may need to see an eye doctor, also called an ophthalmologist. If you have to see a specialist, don't be afraid. They're always trying to help you and wouldn't cause you any harm. • Damian

★ Just remember you have the right to ask questions about your health. • Josie

DRUGS – A habit-forming medicinal substance

 Drugs are a NOOOO! Think about it, would you like to screw up your life because of one little tablet/cigarette/needle? Just don't do it. It's stupid. I never touched the stuff, and I plan to never touch it. If you get offered any, just say no. If it's your friends who offer it to you, and they persist (a real friend wouldn't hassle you about it), don't accept it and seriously consider ending the friendship. • Damian

★ Yes, well, I won't go too much into the drug lecturing. I'm sure you have enough of it from home and school. If you have a problem with any addictive drugs and would like help, there is lots of help available: drug line, doctor, school counselor, and so on. • Josie

ECCENTRIC/ODD – Out of the ordinary, unusual

Anything odd is basically anything that appears different from what is considered normal or average. It can also be called "weird." If you are called weird, think of yourself as a special edition of something; people who call you weird are just jealous that they aren't special editions! I feel odd or different nearly all the time. I sometimes feel I'm living on a different plane of existence than everyone else. Knowing I'm different from everyone else makes me smile because who wants 100 Fords when you can have a Ferrari? • Damian

Some characteristics of AS can make you appear odd/eccentric because of special behaviors and different ways of thinking. For example, if you have a keen interest in science fiction and you love Dr. Who, and you know everything there is to know about Dr. Who, and this is what you talk about, draw about and read about ALL the time, this may appear a little odd to non-Asperger people. Not only because they aren't that interested in Dr. Who, but because they tend to have more of a balance in their special interests. A lot of artistic people are seen as odd or eccentric; this may be because they are so focused on their art. They have very special traits just like people with AS. Look at Einstein, Mozart and Michelangelo – these are famous odd and eccentric people who are suspected of having had AS. Without their eccentricities, we wouldn't have had their science, music or art. What a terrible loss that would have been! • Josie

EMBARRASSING MOMENTS – Awkward times

We all get embarrassed sometimes. Usually, it is from doing something stupid in front of a lot of people, or from someone exposing some information about us. If you do something embarrassing in front of someone who doesn't know you, or who you're never going to see again, then it doesn't matter. If someone says something true but embarrassing about you in front of people you know, then try to justify yourself. Explain why what they said is true. If that

doesn't work, just walk away, because if they are people who aren't your friends, it doesn't really matter. If they are people who are your friends, they wouldn't reject you or do anything negative after hearing what the other person said. An example of an embarrassing moment of my life – MOM FOUND CONDOMS IN MY BAG! I remember walking up to her and noticed my bag was in her hand. She was just talking normally to me and then she said, "By the way, next time hide your condoms better." I was soooo embarrassed. • Damian

Ahem … I was embarrassed too, Damian! Not that I go through Damian's bag for no reason; we were in Italy on vacation, and we were re-sorting all our stuff so we could begin our tour with our individual backpacks. That's when I found them … How super-embarrassing for ME! But on a serious note, I was very pleased that Damian saw the importance of using condoms as protection if he is going to be sexually active. But that's a whole other subject. Other parents and families may feel differently about this. • Josie

EMOTIONS – Any specific feeling such as love, hate, anger and sadness

Emotions are going to affect you your entire life. They will change the decisions you make and your opinions on things. To be honest, the most popular (but not most loved by others) emotions of mine are anger and sadness. Because I've learned to deal with them, I have become emotionally stronger. Whenever something emotionally painful comes up (for example, if you get teased at school, your girlfriend dumps you, and so on), it will change you. At first it may seem bad, but in the long run emotions are good; they teach you how to be strong and deal with things in the future. • Damian

Emotions are strong feelings. Some people with AS have difficulty recognizing emotions or knowing the difference between each emotion. For example, there are lots of degrees of emotions between calm and mad, but

some people with AS go very quickly from one to the other and don't notice the range of emotions that you can experience in between. You may also become confused when other people have very strong emotions.

You can get help in recognizing the stages of emotions through counseling; there are now also some computer programs that teach you how to recognize emotions – your own and those of others. • Josie

EMPATHY – The understanding of another person's emotions or feelings

Empathy basically means being sympathetic to others. I find that I tend to have a lack of empathy. When I see someone in pain, I think of it as something they need to go through to become stronger. When my friend was having major trouble with his girlfriend, I told him it was something he had to go through. I do sympathize with some people, such as people with ASD and any other disability (mental or physical), but I find it hard to sympathize with people without it. Maybe I think that we are the only true victims? I don't know; all I know is that my empathy is mixed up! If this is the case with you, never say that you don't care! People will hate you. • Damian

Well, "hate" is a strong word, Damian; they may not hate you, but they will think you are uncaring or insensitive because they don't understand that some people can lack empathy. A lack of empathy can be a characteristic of AS. So there may be times when you don't understand why somebody is sad or upset about something, because you can't feel what he or she is feeling. Maybe you could practice empathy by thinking of a situation where somebody was emotional or upset and then pretending you were that person and that it had happened to you; how would you feel about the same situation? For example, how would you feel if the thing that is most important to you is taken away forever? Would you feel mad/sad/angry/scared? If you struggle with empathy, then I think the best thing may be to just be neutral or to learn about empathy from a special teacher or counselor. • Josie

ENEMIES – People you hate and are hostile towards

Enemies are basically people who are your rivals or people you hate. You can have an enemy and not hate the person, which would then be a rival. My mom says that having enemies is bad and that you shouldn't have enemies; maybe she's right. There was a time when I had no enemies. I was yearning for one for some excitement in my life, but then when I got one, I didn't really feel happy about it. My advice? Try not to have enemies, but if you have them, try not to feed the hate or the rivalry. • Damian

Yes, as Damian already knows, I think "hate" is a wasted emotion. Just because you don't like somebody or the things a person does, doesn't mean that the person is automatically your enemy. Just because somebody isn't your friend, it doesn't mean he or she is your enemy. People with AS sometimes see every situation as black or white. So it's either "hate" or "like." See if you can get into the grey area, where you are just neutral about it all. If uncertain, ask others for help. • Josie

EXAMS – A set of questions in a formal test

When it comes to exams, it's always good to study. If you think you can get a REALLY good mark without studying, then great for you! But it's still good to study. When I was in 8-10 grade, I didn't really study, and I got a high grade anyway. But grades 11 and 12 were tougher, and I had to study. My advice, get study practice during elementary school and during all of high school. If it gets too tough, tell someone; just because you need help with studying doesn't make you stupid. In fact, it's a very smart thing to ask for help with your studies because it's like an investment in your future! You could ask for help from the teacher, another student or even your parents. • Damian

I still think Damian doesn't study enough! He studies the day before an exam, and he still hasn't quite understood that even if you aren't given homework, you still set some time aside each day to go over all your work and textbooks. Studying time is a very important part of the day. It would be a good idea to slot this time into your after-school routine. • Josie

EXERCISE – Physical activity or training

Exercise is nearly always a good thing. If you can, exercise about 30 minutes a day. I joined the school gym with some of my friends, and it's good. If you're considering joining a gym, don't think that other experienced people will laugh at you because you're a beginner; they will actually help you and give you advice. Remember, when it comes to any exercise, start small. And don't push yourself too much, or you can damage your muscles, which is REALLY BAD! • Damian

Damian, I think you did a good job covering this topic. Also remember that a healthy body can help you have a healthy mind. Exercise is also a great stress release. In fact, Damian has been riding his bike recently as an outlet for stress build-up. And, of course, exercise is very beneficial for weight control, helping you stay fit and healthy. • Josie

EYE CONTACT – Visual contact with another person's eyes

When I was younger, people would often say to me, "Look at me when I'm talking to you!" and I always used to think "Why? The floor is so much more interesting!" We will probably never be able to understand the necessity of eye contact, but apparently it's good manners. Now I look people in the eyes when they talk to me because it's a sign of respect. If you do make eye contact with people who are talking to you, don't stare at them like a robot, however; it might make them feel uncomfortable. • Damian

Damian has covered this topic extremely well. Yes, when he was younger, we were told to encourage him to give us eye contact. But I didn't realize that when he is trying to give eye contact, he couldn't truly listen at the same time. So now instead of asking for eye contact, which is generally considered a sign that somebody is paying attention, I just keep asking if he's listening to me. If you are a person who doesn't like eye contact, it may be a good thing to let people in your life know about this, and reassure them that you are listening even if you are not maintaining eye contact. • Josie

F

FAMILY – A group of people who are related to each other

 Your family is basically your relatives. You can rely on your family for any support you need. Your sibling(s) may be another story. If your siblings annoy you, never become physically violent. If they've annoyed you and continue to annoy you, don't seek revenge. Your parents will eventually realize that you're not doing anything wrong. If it continues, try to stay away from your siblings. Your siblings will get frustrated because they won't have anyone around to blame for anything, and when they do scream you'll be away from them, so there's no way for them to blame you. Take that, Chiara! (my sister). • Damian

I'm not getting into this topic. I believe that a mother should not interfere too much. As a parent I can mediate between my two children. I have to stay neutral about the situation and try to be a type of judge; I cannot take sides, but I can offer some solutions and try to make suggestions that help both of them. • Josie

FASHION – Clothing styles that are the latest craze

Fashion? When it comes to fashion, who cares about what others think? I mean, sure, it's nice to have people comment on how good you look, but that's not necessary. It only matters if you feel good yourself and enjoy what you wear. Don't wear something you hate just because it's popular; if you personally think it's good, then wear it. But, when it comes to fancy things and stuff (like a wedding or something, or maybe you're just going out), a certain dress code may be expected, so in that case, it would be a good idea to ask your parents about what to wear. BE FOREWARNED! Your parents may not have any fashion sense! Once I told my dad I wanted some corduroy pants. He told me he had two pairs and that I could have them. I put them on, thought they looked good, and went out in them. When I came home, Mom saw them and said, "No, you didn't wear them out, did you?" I said "What do you mean?" and she said "OH MY GOSH, ARE YOU SERIOUS? THEY ARE DISCO CORDS FROM THE 80'S!" I was so embarrassed, and I got angry with my dad and also my sister, who claims to be a fashion expert and who didn't tell me they looked bad. • Damian

Damian is still learning about clothing combinations – mixing and matching tops with bottoms. Once you learn a few combinations, then you will be fine. Maybe take some photos of combinations and have them handy for reference. If you want to follow fashions, look at magazines or watch the people you admire and what they wear. But be cautioned, if they are expensive brands, you may need to get a job to pay for it! You can buy equivalent-looking clothing at cheaper stores. Some people with Asperger Syndrome don't like the feel of certain clothing, material, and so on. For example, if you only like elastic waists, then go with how you feel, not with fashion. Create your own fashion! • Josie

FEAR – A feeling of anxiety, uneasiness and nervousness

Fears are normal. Fears nearly always have a good reason behind them. I personally have a fear of heights; the reason for that is obvious (splat). I remember at school camp when we were doing the high ropes, another student said that if I'm afraid of heights, then I'm actually afraid of the ground because that's what I'm afraid to hit. So the best solution is to get away from the ground and go as high as possible so you can't see it. It makes sense, but it still didn't help. But if I ever go high, I assure myself of my safety by making sure I won't fall. If you have a fear, you can either hide from it or confront it. The best option is not the same every time. Sometimes it's best to confront it; sometimes it's best to hide from it. That is up to you to decide, but confronting your fears is not always wise (for example, if you're afraid of a homicidal murderer, it's not a good idea to confront the murderer). • Damian

Sometimes it's unfamiliarity with things that makes us afraid of them. For example, I used to be scared of snakes, but a friend of mine owns snakes and has educated me about them and I'm not afraid of them any more, even though I am very careful around them. If you have a strong fear of something or somebody, talk to an adult. He or she may be able to relieve your fear by talking about it, sharing written and other materials about it, etc. • Josie

FIGHT – A physical struggle or battle

Fighting is a weird thing to talk about. Fights are different from a teenager's versus a kid's perspective. Sometimes people start fights when they're defending their honor (honor of a girlfriend/boyfriend, honor of a friend or themselves). Sometimes they fight to prey on the weak (these are like bullies), or they fight for fun or because they just feel like it. My advice is not to start a fight. However, if someone attacks you, then self-defense is compulsory! My principal once told a friend of mine that he wasn't allowed to fight

with anyone, not even in self-defense. He was just supposed to take the beating. This order from the principal was wrong. If you are a victim, you must defend yourself, or you may be seriously hurt. If you feel like fighting someone because you are angry with that person, my advice is to deal with your anger in some other way. I've wanted to fight so many people, even violently at times. But I took my anger out in a nonviolent way. A few years ago, someone insulted my girlfriend at the time. I wanted to smash his face in, but I didn't. I just crippled his reputation. Basically, I made everyone turn against him by telling everyone stuff that he had done and how he wasn't a very good person. I have fought people over the years, but I'm proud to say that I haven't fought anyone in high school. • Damian

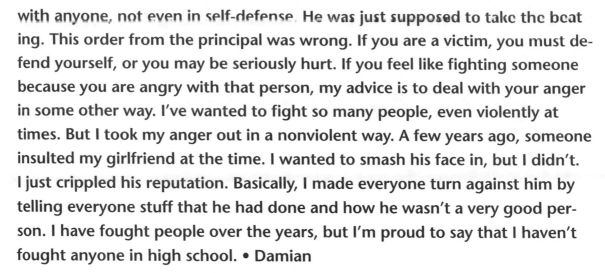Hmm, I don't agree with Damian. I think violence should be avoided at all times. The best thing to do in a fight situation is to be the better person … and walk away. If the person who wants to fight you follows you and corners you so you aren't able to escape, that is a different matter. Try to talk your way out of the situation; if this still is not successful and the person becomes physical with you, then it becomes a case of self-defense. It would be good to learn some safety strategies for what to do if you are in a situation like that. Also, depending on the situation, go to an adult or the police for help. • Josie

FORGIVENESS – To stop resenting or being angry with someone

Forgiveness can be hard both to give and to receive. If you are the one who's done something wrong, my advice is to say you're sorry and ask what you can do to make up for it. If they tell you to do something bad, like do an illegal or immoral favor to make up for it, don't even think about it. Obviously, they're not worth the trouble of forgiveness. If someone else has done something bad to you, it can be hard to forgive, depending on what it was they did. But remember that if you forgive someone, it makes you a better person. Don't let anyone force you to say sorry if you don't mean it. Once this girl asked me out to dinner, but then some random guy asked her out and she said yes and dumped our dinner date. I was so mad. After about a month or two I got a text message from her saying she was sorry. I told her how it made me feel, but I also told her I forgave her. A forgiving person is a good person. • Damian

 I agree with Damian; forgiving somebody releases you from any negative feelings. Also, if you hate somebody and don't forgive the person, you are actually giving him or her your "power." So take back your "power" by forgiving. • Josie

FRIENDSHIP – Companionship, bonding, being friends, fellowship

Friendship is a bond between two people who like each other but not necessarily in a romantic way. Apparently, a friend is a lot harder to find as you get older, so try to get as many friends as possible while you're young. A lot of people I know complain that in elementary school they had like tons of friends, but now they don't have very many. I personally find this weird, because in my elementary school I had three friends but now in senior high school I have about 20. Elementary school students are usually a lot more immature and crueler because they don't understand too much (no offense to anyone in elementary school).

Anyway, when it comes to making friends, it can be easier than it seems. In class if you sit next to someone new, maybe start to talk to them and find if you like them or not. If you do, become more and more friendly over time. I find (from my sister) that it is a lot easier for girls to make friends, but guys are a lot more exclusive. There will be some points in your life when you might have a fight with one or several of your friends. If so, it is healthy to try to sort it out with them as soon as possible. If you don't end the trouble soon, the temporary dislike of you can become permanent. Friends look out for each other, help each other, socialize with each other, and even sometimes joke and trade friendly insults with each other. These friendly insults are just jokes and are supposed to be funny for everyone, including the victim of the joke. Friends usually have known each other for a long time, which means that they have gotten along with each other for so long, which is what makes them friends. Friends may also be friends because of similar interests and hobbies. For example, some of my friends and I share an interest in computers. Some of my friendships were made because I was in the same class. Similar people get along! My first elementary school friend became my friend because we had the same name. My second friend I met through him. I've noticed that now I meet most of my friends through other friends. It's a bit like the expression "any friend of yours is a friend of mine!"

A fact you must know is that friends don't like to be the victims of obsession. Don't obsess over friendship. Don't get paranoid if a friend doesn't pick up the phone when you try calling; don't get worried if a friend needs his own space. It doesn't mean he doesn't want to be your friend. If your friend tells you to do stupid things, don't do them. Sometimes supposed friends might use you to do stupid things for them or for their own amusement. These types of people are not friends. True friends look out for each other. They help each other but do not tell each other to do stupid things that might get you into trouble or danger. • Damian

 A friendship is something you have between yourself and a buddy, mate or pal – people you feel close to and can be yourself with who aren't your family. You will have many different types of friendships throughout your life. Some will last a few weeks, months, years or even a lifetime. Your friends are all different; some you see every day at school, some on the weekends, and some friends you might catch up with every few months. If you draw a circle with four inner rings, then you can mark your friends in the circle according to how close they are to you; for example, the friends on the innermost circle are your closest friends, and the friends on the outside circle are the ones you catch up with once in a while.

We need to look after our friendships; They are like a garden: They need nurturing and weeding. Every friendship has its ups and downs. Be yourself, and if a friend doesn't like you any more, let him or her go. If a friend complains

to you about your behavior, don't be defensive. Think about what your friend has said; if you are confused, talk to another friend or an adult about it. Maybe there is something that you can improve on; ask for help and learn about it. Enjoy your friends, but don't become too dependent on them as that may push them away. Finally, you may not feel a need for friends. That is fine, too. There is no right or wrong. Learn to enjoy your own company and be your own best friend! • Josie

FUN – Joy, happy, amusing, pleasant, entertaining times

Something fun is something you enjoy. The more fun you have in your life, the more of your life you enjoy. Unfortunately, there are many times in life that will not be fun. This is something that everyone must deal with. But sometimes doing things that are not fun will have a reward afterwards. The reward can be anything from money, to a really clean room (from tidying your room, which is usually not very fun), to a good feeling inside from helping someone. Never expect a reward though, because you may be disappointed. One of the most fun times of my life was when my school went on a ski trip. The bus ride was exciting, skiing was lots of fun, and I was with my mates all week! I really enjoyed it. • Damian

Glad you can see the positive in cleaning your room, Damian. Having fun is also a way to relax and enjoy your life. You can have fun with your friends, family, pets, computer game or yourself. It's important to have a balance in your life, so if life is too serious and heavy – like you are feeling sad a lot, or you have a lot of school work – then make sure you slot in some fun time. Think of the things that bring you pleasure or that make you laugh or smile. • Josie

GOALS – Something you want to aim for

A goal is something that you want to achieve. Goals are vital for moving on in life. If you have a big goal that you wish to accomplish, I suggest you set little goals that end up achieving the main one. This way, whenever you finish a smaller goal, you get a good feeling from finishing it, and that gives you enthusiasm to finish the next one. For example, I want a successful career in science. So my first goal was to get a traineeship in science. My next goal was to get into a university, and so on. Smaller goals can be saving up for that cool new computer game or trying to swim 50 laps. • Damian

I think Damian has given a very good example of goals and goal setting. • Josie

GOSSIP – Whispering, rumor, scandalous talk

Gossip is small talk, rumors and stuff. It's not nice to gossip about people, though I have to admit that I do it sometimes; most people do. At my school, I do more listening than passing it on. I have to remember not to think that it is all true. People did a little gossip about me when someone typed my name in Google and found information on Asperger and me. People were like "What? What's this?" and there was a little talking going around; nothing big. I just ignored it. • Damian

To know the difference between gossip and non-gossip, ask yourself, "Would I say this to the person's face?" If you wouldn't, but you would say it to somebody else, then it's probably gossip. For example, I complain to a friend, "Damian is so annoying; his room is always untidy and so messy." Because this is something that I always tell Damian anyhow, to his face, it isn't gossip. But if I said to a friend, "Damian is such a pain; I wish he'd move out," and this is something I wouldn't say to Damian's face, then it is gossip. You may be very literal and truly believe what people tell you. It is quite common for persons with Asperger Syndrome to be very black and white in their thinking. When in doubt, ask a good friend or an adult to help you sort things out. • Josie

GUILT – A feeling of having done something bad or wrong, self-blame

Guilt is a bad feeling you get when you know you've done something wrong. It's like a self-punishment. When I was about 5 or 6 years old, I accidentally cut my sweater with my scissors. I was too afraid to tell my mom, so I told her that someone else had done it. At school the next day, the kid I blamed got into so much trouble because my mom had called school. After that I felt REALLY guilty because I realized that I was protecting myself and in the process had gotten someone else into trouble. I think it took me about 6 months before I got the guts to admit it to my mom. When I did, she got upset with me, but then again, it was the least I deserved. My advice, if you are certain that what you have done is wrong, give in to your guilt and admit it. It will clear your conscience, and you will feel better. • Damian

Good example, Damian. Guilt is a feeling that's inside your body, and it comes up when you are feeling bad and feeling that something is your fault or that you are to blame for something. It's okay to feel it, but don't dwell on it. Instead, do something about it. Admit your mistake, make amends, and get over it. • Josie

HARASSMENT – Repeated abuse, torment or attacks

Harassment is a bit like annoyance, only at an extreme level. In eighth grade there was a student who was harassing my friends and me. We got so irritated that we ended up hating the guy. We told our teachers, and they eventually stopped it. If you get in the same position, tell the person to stop, or report it to an adult. • Damian

There are two sides to this topic. Also be aware if you are harassing somebody else. If you are a little obsessed about a friend and are contacting him or her all the time, either by phone, email or text message, sometimes it can be seen as harassment – especially if that person doesn't like all the contact. If you are worried that you may be harassing somebody, ask an adult for advice or help before it goes too far. Conversely, if you feel that somebody is harassing you, then ask him or her to stop; if they don't, talk to an adult. Serious harassment can even lead to trouble with the police. • Josie

HATE – Strong feeling of dislike, disgust or hostility

Hate is the opposite of love. There are quite a number of people I "hate." Just because you hate someone, you don't have to express it to them. But it is good sometimes to do so, but not in a violent way. If you hold in your hate and pretend you like someone, you are just being fake and not being your true self. • Damian

Yes, it's okay not to like somebody, but if you don't like him or her, wouldn't it make sense not to have anything to do with that person? Hate is a negative emotion; if you feel a lot of hate for somebody, you are actually giving that person power over you. Take your own power back by not spending so much hate energy on others. If you need to process or express the hatred, then write about it, or speak to an adult or a counselor. Then move on to things and people who bring you joy. • Josie

HEALTH – A fit and vital condition of mind and body

 Health is extremely important to your general well-being. EAT YOUR VEGETABLES! When I was younger, my parents would tell me that certain things or behaviors were healthy, and I didn't know how important health was. I look back now and think, "Gee, my parents were right; I will thank them when I'm older." I love vegetables now, especially in Pepperonata! YUUM! (An Italian vegetable dish, like a stew.) • Damian

A balanced diet is the key to good health. Unless you have certain allergies or food sensitivities, a little bit of everything is what your body needs. If you think of your body as a car and food as fuel, then you can see that it's important to put good food into your body for it to run properly. • Josie

HEARTBREAK – Overwhelming grief, disappointment or sorrow

Getting your heart broken is very hard to deal with. It can last a very long time, even months! I was in love with a girl, and when she left me, it took me a long time to deal with the pain. I felt very mixed up – I hated her, I wanted to be friends with her, wanted her to die, wanted to get back with her; it was confusing, but over time it healed. • Damian

There's no set time for a heart to heal; everyone's grieving process is different. But if you are really depressed about it and feel like you can't go on with life, or feel like you want to hurt somebody, or yourself, then you may need to get some help in moving on. Talk to an adult or your counselor. • Josie

HELP – Gaining assistance to make things easier

Help is like assistance. It is important to be able to accept help, and sometimes it is even more important to help someone else. Be careful though; never expect someone whom you have helped to help you in return. There have been many times where I have helped someone (maybe helped them with homework or lent them money), but when I needed their help, they told me to get stuffed. It was then that I coined the phrase "Helpers never get helped," but actually that is not always true. Nice people will help you in return, and even nicer people will help you anyway. • Damian

I believe that if you help someone without expecting something in return, then you won't be disappointed if nothing is returned! Helping somebody should be done because you want to – not because you want something in return. So ask yourself when you are helping somebody, "Why am I doing this?" Also, it's okay to ask others for help if you don't understand something or are feeling overwhelmed by a task. Asking for help doesn't mean there's something wrong with you or that you have failed. Just the opposite can be true: It means you are wise and looking after yourself, because you are supporting yourself by asking others to help out. • Josie

HOBBY – An activity or special interest to do in your spare time

Hobbies are things or activities that we are interested in. For example, I am interested in playing the piano, so that is one of my hobbies. It is good to have hobbies because they make your life enjoyable. But be aware that it is not healthy to spend too much of your time with your hobbies. About two years ago, my favorite hobby was computers; I would play on my computer for hours and all I would think about was computers. I was obsessed! But I then realized there was other fun stuff to do, like playing a sport, watching TV or going to the movies, because I noted other kids at school were doing those things. Ultimately, playing the piano is one of my hobbies. Playing a musical instrument is very rewarding. If you're looking for a hobby, I suggest a musical instrument. • Damian

Yes, Damian is right, hobbies are for self-entertainment and are ways of relaxing and diverting your mind. Hobbies are also a great way to get to know people and possibly gain new friendships. But if your hobby begins to take over your life, for example, if you are constantly thinking of it or doing it, that is not a healthy balance; that is an obsession. People with AS are prone to having obsessions, so if you think you may be obsessed with a hobby, try to come up with ways to balance it out. • Josie

HOMEWORK – Assignments, study, classwork or lessons completed at home

Homework ... great ... how exciting; not! I believe homework is a time waster because everything you're supposed to learn at school should be taught at school. But if we want to get an education, then we must follow the school's rules. If you do your homework, you might learn more about the subjects, so do your homework on a regular basis! • Damian

If you find that you are so stressed and tired when you get home that you just can't, or don't have time to, do your homework, talk to your parents or teachers about the situation. Perhaps some special arrangements can be made to lessen or avoid homework. • Josie

HOMOSEXUAL – Sexual desire for somebody of the same gender

I don't like it when people insult homosexuals or "gays," as people like to call them. It really pisses me off. It's like being racist. Hating someone for no real reason. If you think that you are a homosexual, then that is okay. If people tease or bully you about it, you need to decide how to deal with it. If necessary, get advice from an adult. Don't be afraid if you think you are turning "gay," because there is usually at least once in every person's life when they think that they might be turning homosexual. Don't be afraid of it; what's there to be afraid about? And as for what I have said before about people insulting gays, don't do it; it really is stupid. It is just a reaction from fear of being gay yourself. • Damian

 Your sexual orientation is extremely personal. It doesn't have anything to do with anybody else. If you are confused about your sexuality, don't get stressed about it. Talk to a professional who may help you with your decisions. Talking to your parents is great too, but often it can be embarrassing. • Josie

HORMONES – Substances/chemicals produced in parts of the body

Um … I'm a guy, so I don't know much about this. Maybe testosterone, but even with that I only really know that it is a name for a male hormone, and that's about it. • Damian

Males and females have lots of different hormones. They play big parts in our body, like instruments in a band. Sometimes they are out of balance, and that's when they can create disharmony in our bodies. Things like hormones can cause acne and mood swings. In extreme cases, hormonal imbalances can have more serious effects on your body and mind. If you are further interested, do some research on the Internet or at the library. • Josie

HYGIENE – Cleanliness and sanitation

Hygiene is very important. You may not realize just how important hygiene is. I used to take 30-second showers, and I only now realize how bad that was! It just wasn't time enough to get clean and freshened up. And brushing your teeth – extremely important. I used to brush my teeth, oh – maybe once a month or two – but then my teeth started to hurt. My mom and the dentist told me what could happen when you don't brush on a regular basis, like infections and cavities. So brush your teeth twice a day, especially before you go to bed. Flossing is important to dental care too. Also, don't forget to wash your hands after going to the toilet. I know it seems like a ton of rules, but it's for your own good and everyone else's health. Imagine being about 30 years of age or maybe even younger and getting all your teeth replaced because you never brushed them and thinking, "if only I had listened to everyone." • Damian

 Very WISE advice, Damian. Unfortunately, it usually takes Damian experiencing the negative before he learns. When I used to nag him about his teeth, he didn't believe me. It had to get to the stage where his teeth and gums hurt, his breath was rancid and the dentist could see early signs of potential decay! If you are unsure about hygiene and want some help, ask a friend or an adult about how often bathing is recommended, and so on. Proper hygiene also includes changing your clothes on a regular basis, wearing clean clothes, washing and combing your hair, and so on. • Josie

INDEPENDENCE – Freedom to choose and live as you like

Independence is what teenagers LOVE! But, subconsciously, we seem to still be childish, and sometimes without knowing it, yearn for non-independence. It's really weird, and you would have to go into all of that psychiatric stuff to explain it. The main point of independence is that eventually you will have to be fully independent. It is good to practice to act as responsibly as you can, because the more you practice, the easier it will be for you as an adult. • Damian

★ I agree, Damian. Teenagers want to be independent but also still crave guidance from adults. This is all a normal part of growing up. There are benefits to independence and also consequences of independence. If you want to be "grown up," you need to make adult decisions and be responsible for your decisions even if they go wrong sometimes. • Josie

INSULT – Offense, abuse, threat or speaking with disrespect

🌀 An insult is like an offense, as when someone calls you names or something. Usually bullies like to do this (see Bully). Sometimes people insult each other as a joke. Like with some of my friends, we insult each other all the time, jokingly. But when someone insults you and you're not sure if it's a joke or not, all you have to do is look at his facial expression to see if he really means what he says. I know that can be difficult for those of us on the spectrum, but keep the following in mind: If the person insulting you is laughing or has a friendly, smiling face, it was probably a joke. If he has an aggressive, angry-looking face, assume that it was a proper insult. All you should do is either ignore them or insult them back. Sometimes ignoring them is the best because if it doesn't bother you, then it is a waste of their time and breath. Also ignore them if you can't tell what their facial expression is. • Damian

★ Exactly, Damian. Insults are a form of bullying, whether you are being insulted or you are insulting somebody. • Josie

INTELLIGENT – Clever, bright, smart or gifted

🌀 Intelligent means smart. It's a good thing. I find it funny when people call intelligent people "nerds" just because they're smart. To me, it shows that they're jealous! (see Jealousy) But if you are smart, don't always try to correct people. There's someone at my school who always does that, and it can get REALLY annoying. Also, don't push your opinions on others; be open-minded about answers or information. • Damian

★ Many people with AS are very intelligent, particularly in math and science or about a special interest of theirs. Be proud of your intelligence, but like Damian says, you don't need to brag about it. People already know you are intelligent, so you don't need to prove it. • Josie

INTERNET – A worldwide computer network

The Internet is the thing that connects all the computers in the world together, like a network. You probably already know what the Internet is, but remember NOT to open .exe files that you have downloaded off the Internet unless you have scanned them for viruses or Trojans (this is the file viruses use). I know this because my friend gave me a program once that makes a little Trojan (like something that sends passwords and information from your computer to the source of the Trojan), and it needed to be merged with an .exe file. Also, never assume that what you are being told over the Internet is true; although the Internet is very useful and a good way to communicate with people, look up information and play games, not all information you find posted is correct and not all people you come in contact with are who they pretend to be. Never reveal too much about yourself, including telephone number and home address, and when in doubt, consult with an adult. • Damian

★ I agree, the Internet is a wonderful thing but it is also an open window to lots of negatives, such as viruses and people trying to take advantage of you. If you are unsure about someone or something over the Internet, get advice. If you find that you are on the Internet 24/7, you may be becoming obsessed about it. Try to find a balance. Work out how many hours you are spending on the computer and take lots of breaks and fit in other activities. • Josie

JEALOUSY – Possessiveness, suspicion, envy and resentment

Jealousy is when you don't like someone because you want something they have or you want something that happened to them to happen to you. Envy is different; it's when you just want to have what somebody has or want the thing that happened to them to happen to you, but without disliking them. A lot of people can't admit they are jealous. Because they can't admit they are jealous, they like to accuse others of being jealous just to get a reaction. If someone calls you jealous, just agree with them because then they fail to get a reaction. Like if my friend gets a new cell phone and he tries to show it off and call me jealous, I'll just agree and say that it's a nice phone. If I agree, it means I have no issue with it, so then my friend can't tease me. I have been jealous of many people because they have gotten what they do not deserve. I'm not jealous any more though, because I know that I shouldn't compare what I have to what others have. • Damian

Good points, Damian. Yes, jealousy is a negative emotion that can eat away at you. It is a desire to have what another has. For example, if you are jealous of your girlfriend when she talks to another guy – it's because you are afraid of losing her to somebody else. If your jealousy is out of hand and you are possessive about someone or something, it might help you to talk to somebody about it. Get some perspective on the situation. If you are happy about yourself and what you have in life, you can be envious of somebody once in a while. Envy is a healthier type of jealousy – where you think, "Wow, lucky them; wish it was me," but then move on. • Josie

JOB – A task, duty or employment, work, occupation or profession

A job is a moneymaker! If you want money, you have to do or give something in return. Right now I've got a job in a laboratory as a trainee.

It's really cool, and I enjoy my work. If you go to a job interview and wonder what to wear, I suggest you wear either what you normally wear to school or maybe nice casual clothes. Don't go to the interview with dirty clothes or really casual or inappropriate stuff. But it isn't necessary to wear a suit; that's only for huge careers in big business or something. Remember, if you don't get the job, don't get upset because there are a million other jobs out there. A job is similar to a career (see Careers). • Damian

Spot on, Damian. But there's more to it than wearing the right clothes to the interview, even if that is also important. If you are keen to get a job, then ask adults – parents, teachers, counselors, family members, neighbors, etc. – for advice on how to start. You don't just walk up to somebody and ask for a job; there is a sequence of events leading up to this. Write up a resumé, ask people to be references (this is where a person will speak positively about you to a prospective employer), look for job vacancies, apply for the job and, if you are asked to come in for an interview, prepare for and attend the interview.

Once you have been given a job, there are rules and regulations just like at school, so make sure you learn about them. Lots of books have been written on this subject; you might want to check some of them out. A good idea is to do some volunteer work. This will give you experience so you can write the work down on your resumé. Volunteer work could be helping out at the elderly home, helping a charity, or cutting lawns. • Josie

JOKES – Anything said or done to bring on laughter

Jokes are basically things that people do or say to get laughs. Sometimes people joke about each other. This can be extremely funny, but if you joke about others too much, it can get offensive. It depends on what or who is being joked about. If I think that something is offensive, but at the same time know that it was a joke, I look semi-offended instead of laughing. My friends used to call me an idiot as a joke all the time, but they could see by the expression on my face that I didn't like it, so they stopped.

If you have trouble showing that you don't like something, then just say so nicely. This usually makes the person making the joke feel guilty and he probably won't do it again. Of course, if the person who is joking about you is not your friend and is someone who doesn't like you, this approach probably won't work. If they keep doing it, it turns into bullying (see Bullying). I remember in sixth grade, the girls knew who I had a crush on and they'd play "jokes" on me. The girl I liked would come up to me with food in her mouth and say "will you go out with me?" to mock me. I look back now and think how stupid were they? • Damian

Joking between friends is okay, but only if both people are laughing. It's not okay to purposely tease someone and then try to cover yourself by saying, ''I was only joking!'' when you have hurt somebody's feelings. And vice versa – it's not okay for others to excuse their bullying behaviors by saying, "We were only joking." A joke is only a joke when both parties are in on it. A joke is also a funny anecdote with a punch line.

Sometimes people with AS don't understand the meaning of a joke. If you find yourself in that situation and you feel comfortable admitting it, admit it, and maybe the joke will be explained to you. If you don't feel safe to say you didn't "get" the joke, in most cases the best thing is to just laugh along with everyone. • Josie

JOURNAL – A book for writing about your daily activities or recording your feelings

A journal is a great way to express how you feel. It's a book in which you basically write how you feel about certain things and stuff that you don't want to tell anyone but still want to express. I had a journal, and it was useful for me. I don't use it much any more; I write poems now about my feelings. A lot of people find poems hard, especially if they hate English (the subject), so it might be better if you just use a journal. You can also use an online blog, but they usually aren't private, so it's not very good for secrets. • Damian

 I think Damian explained everything about what a journal is. • Josie

KINDNESS – The act of being considerate, generous, helpful and thoughtful

Kindness basically means being nice to people. It is a good thing to show kindness, because if you're kind, people will like you. Be as kind as you can, without letting people take advantage of your kindness. Some people who are mean, such as bullies (see Bully), may take advantage of your kindness and make or influence you to do things that they make sound helpful when, really, they'll hurt someone or benefit themselves but no one else. Sometimes it is hard to find out what people's real intentions are, but if you get the slightest suspicion that somebody might be using you, investigate it; ask people who have a neutral position. If the person who is possibly "using" you is a bully, or was a bully, it is urgent that you find out what he really wants. Sometimes bullies pretend not to be bullies just to backstab their victims. • Damian

 Hmm, yes, Damian, I agree that it is a nice thing to be kind to all, and yes I agree that sometimes people can take advantage of your kindness. If you can learn how to "read" people's facial and body language, then you will be more equipped to deal with these situations. Once again "reading" people's facial and body language is a difficult thing for persons with Asperger Syndrome to do. You can be taught some of these skills within some social understanding classes or, if unsure, ask somebody. • Josie

KISSING – When one person's lips touch another person's lips

 Kissing is something people like to do when they have feelings for each other. It is basically when people press their lips together. More can be done in kissing, such as the use of tongue. The feelings that are present when people kiss can be different every time. It can be a love feeling (see Love), or it can be a feeling of lust, which is more sexual than love. I suggest that if you want to kiss a girl, you prepare yourself and go over the situation first in your mind. If you and the person you want to kiss are together as a dating couple, then it is probably appropriate. If you are not together, it is inappropriate to kiss if the person doesn't feel the same way. You can never just go up to someone and kiss without warning, because not only is that scary to the person you kissed, it is also socially unacceptable. In fact, it can be illegal because it can be seen as harassment. • Damian

Very good advice, Damian. If you want to learn more or practice kissing, watch movies – and see lots of different types of kissing – soft, hard, quick, long, and so on. Don't be too nervous or stressed out when you are going to kiss; just relax, and it will come naturally to you. There are different types of kissing, from a kiss on the cheek for your grandmother to a romantic kiss for your girlfriend. Ultimately, if you don't want to do it, don't! • Josie

LAZY – Idle, sluggish, loafing, careless, weary and tired

 Being lazy basically means you don't really want to do anything. Usually if you feel lazy, you feel tired or just can't be bothered to do something, or simply want to be left alone. Being lazy isn't a good thing; if people call you lazy, it can be hurtful. I advise that you try not to be lazy, but if you want to be lazy, be my guest. (P.S.: I'm lazy!) • Damian

⭐ A lack of motivation can also be seen as being lazy; for example, you don't want to get up to go to school, you just want to sit on the couch and watch TV for days and do nothing, or you don't feel like doing anything new or exciting. You may be physically unhealthy, and this can come across as being sluggish and lazy. Being a teenager means your body and mind are still growing; besides, you have a lot to do, like school, homework, etc. This all makes you very tired, so sometimes lazy can be mistaken for being tired. If you are always being accused of being lazy, do you want to change? If so, think about why and what is going on – is it for physical or emotional reasons? If so, then get some help. Otherwise, you may have to develop a plan for getting involved in things – and stick to your plan. • Josie

LIE – An intentional untruth, falsehood, inaccurate statement

🌀 A lie is when someone tells another person something that isn't true or provides false information on purpose. If it isn't on purpose, it means that the person telling the false information doesn't know that it is false but believes that it is the truth. This is not a lie. So if someone tells you something that isn't true, don't automatically assume that they are lying. They might just be confused or somehow have gotten incorrect information. You will come across a lot of lying in your life, so it is good to be prepared.

If someone lies but not for a bad reason, it is called a "white lie." This is often done to make sure someone's feelings don't get hurt. For example, if someone asks you to come to play some computer games and you don't want to go because you think the guy's games are not interesting, you might say that you cannot go because you have too much homework. In this case, you use a white lie, not enough time because of homework, instead of saying directly that you don't care for the guy's games and, thereby, avoid hurting his feelings or making him mad.

LI've lied; almost everyone does sooner or later! But I've only hugely lied maybe about three times in my life. The first lie I can remember was in first grade. I was playing with scissors and cut my school sweater. I got scared and thought my mom would get angry with me, so when I got home, I said a classmate did it. Mom called the school. The classmate I accused got into trouble, and his mom had to fix my sweater. I feel bad about that now; it was a stupid thing to do. At this point, I can't do anything about it except to learn from the experience and try not to lie again. • Damian

 Hmm, I remember that, Damian! Sometimes we lie because we don't feel safe telling the truth; this is why Damian lied to me; he was scared I would get angry with him. But, in reality, it's easier to tell the truth because the truth is fact. If you lie, it's hard to remember your lie because it's fiction, and deep down you worry about being found out. People with Asperger Syndrome tend to be quite literal thinkers and, therefore, are usually not tempted to tell lies. However, at the same time, they are often trusting and may not suspect when somebody else is lying – whether it is a "real" lie or a "white" lie. As always, if you are not sure, ask others. Being honest is the safest approach. • Josie

LONELY – Solitary, alone, abandoned and deserted

Being lonely basically means being by yourself. It can also be a feeling (feeling lonely), which can mean that you aren't alone, but you feel like you are. This can mean either exclusion, or emotionally alone (no one to reach out to or no one to love). Most people don't like loneliness, but just because most people like a certain thing doesn't mean it's normal (see Normal). If you like to be alone, that's fine. Some people with AS like to be alone because they find that people can be overwhelming, or they want to be alone because others are mean to them. Sometimes I like to be alone. Maybe at a party or something, halfway through the night I'll just go off by myself to be alone for a little while, maybe 15 minutes. I don't know exactly why I feel that way. • Damian

★ Damian has explained "lonely" very well. I might just add that when Damian says that sometimes he goes off by himself to be alone for 15 minutes, this is probably because it's a chance to unwind and download, so he can then rejoin the party without being overloaded. This is a very good strategy for persons with AS! • Josie

LOVE – Deep affection, infatuation and attachment to a person or thing

🌀 Love is a feeling that people have for each other. It is a strong admiration or a strong liking of someone. There is also another type of love, which is family love. This love usually covers the entire family. Apart from your family, usually you'll love several people in your life; most likely one at a time. This means that you will likely break up with people, or the person you love might leave you, but your family will always be your family. They will always be there for you and will always love you with that special kind of family love. Family love is a LOT harder to break than other types of love. I have loved someone other than a family member; it is a good feeling. Usually when you love somebody, you want to be with that person all the time and your chest hurts when you're not with them. Yes, that may seem dependent like a drug or something and not good, but really, when you're in love, you love it. • Damian

★ Love is an emotion and can be quite complicated. Love is different for everyone, and it's hard to explain. It can be a very deep and tender feeling for a person, creature or an object such as grandparent, music, or a pet; yes, even chocolate! You can show love by caring for that person, creature or object. Unfortunately, sometimes you may love a person, but he or she doesn't love you back. This can feel bad, and you may feel sad or even angry about it. Just remember, you can't make people love you back; it has to happen naturally, so if you love somebody and she doesn't love you, don't try to force her. That can get you into serious trouble, with the police even, because it can be seen as harassment or stalking. If you are sad and confused about love, please talk to somebody about it. Otherwise, love is a good and happy emotion. • Josie

MANNERS – Polite social behavior

Manners are very important. Manners are like showing your respect for someone. When I was younger, I didn't understand what the big deal about respect was, but now I do. Manners make absolutely no sense to most kids, and maybe not even to some teenagers. But manners are very important, because if you are polite and have good manners, people will like you. Being polite and well mannered involves opening the door for people, eating with your mouth closed AND putting the toilet seat down after using it (guys only). Yes, I know! These stupid, annoying things seem meaningless and stupid, but, hey, people like it! So why not do them? • Damian

Manners are part of social behavior, and some people with AS have difficulty with social behavior. But manners are probably one of the easiest forms of social behaviors that you can learn. Once you learn a few manners, they will be easy to use, as they don't change and are consistent. Manners are basically polite behaviors, such as saying "thank you" and "please," opening a door for someone, waiting your turn in line, and so on. • Josie

MEDIATION – The act of negotiation to achieve reconciliation

I used to hate mediation. I used to think it was an act against conflict and I used to LOOOOVE conflict! Not any more. Now I think mediation is good. It shows the view of both sides, and in the end mediation leads to a solution that everyone likes. If everyone is happy, it's a win-win situation. • Damian

★ Yes, mediation is when two people or groups of people can't agree on something and bring in a third person who is neutral on the topic to help them come to an agreement. It allows people to come to a situation, where, like Damian said, everyone is happy. • Josie

MEDITATION – Deep continued thought and reflection

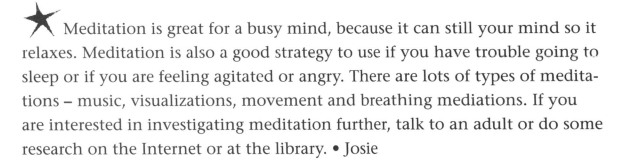 Meditation is like a state of hibernation. You can do this by listening to special meditation CDs while closing your eyes and staying where you are (sitting or lying down). Though this sounds "gypsy voodoo," a little strange, it is actually pretty good to clear your mind, and it is useful for solving emotional problems, calming yourself down, etc. I personally do meditations every now and then, and I find them very relaxing. • Damian

★ Meditation is great for a busy mind, because it can still your mind so it relaxes. Meditation is also a good strategy to use if you have trouble going to sleep or if you are feeling agitated or angry. There are lots of types of meditations – music, visualizations, movement and breathing mediations. If you are interested in investigating meditation further, talk to an adult or do some research on the Internet or at the library. • Josie

METAPHOR – Figure of speech, simile

Metaphors are like figures of speech. They include sayings like "pull up your socks" and "it's raining cats and dogs." "Pull up your socks" means "get on with it," and "it's raining cat's and dogs" means "it's raining really heavily." I was once sitting down and a girl said to me "close your curtains." I was like "what?" I was confused and looked at the windows nearby. When I saw that all curtains were already closed, I was confused even more. Another girl saw that I was confused and whispered, "she means close your legs." I was like "okay ..." because my legs were spread out while I was sitting down. Metaphors never seem logical to me, why not just say what you mean directly? But unfortunately people use them (for some weird reason ...). • Damian

That's interesting, Damian, I wonder why we use metaphors? Metaphors are forms of creative speech, like poetry. If you find metaphors difficult to understand, be honest about it and ask for an explanation – or take note of what was said and investigate it further when you go home, with a family member, or on the Internet or something like that. There are even books on metaphors you can study if you are really interested. Metaphors are difficult for people with AS, who tend to like words to be structured and real, not so creative. If you are faced with a metaphor, try to be creative and imagine what is said. Some examples are:

- "Feeling blue" doesn't mean you are the color blue, it means that maybe you are feeling sad (the color blue has been related to the feeling sad).
- "My plate is already full" doesn't mean that you have a full plate at the dinner table. It means that you have too many things to do and don't have any room for anything else; therefore, a plate is the symbol for a limited space for things. • Josie

MISTAKE – An error, blunder or miscalculation

A mistake is basically when you do something wrong by accident. We all make mistakes because we are human. Even computers make mistakes (especially when they crash or screw up). If you make a mistake, don't get too upset about it, and if people blame you, try to ignore them. Once I was in church and my hand accidentally hit a bottle of holy wine that was on a table and made it spill all over the floor. Everyone was angry with me, yelling and stuff, and I got all upset and felt so guilty. What made it even worse was that they didn't even give me a chance to help clean it up, because immediately everyone started crowding around and cleaning it up. When I look back at it now, I laugh. It's almost funny! If it is something relatively minor like this, just say, "Oh well, stuff happens" and move on. • Damian

★ I agree, Damian; a mistake is like an accident. The great thing is you can learn from your mistakes, and then move on. Maybe Damian learned from that mistake to be more careful when he is in an important place. Also, when we make a mistake, it's a good thing to either clear it up, clean it up or make up for it. As Damian says, he wasn't given a chance, but his intention was to do so. • Josie

MOBILE PHONE (CELL PHONE) – Portable telephone

If you have a mobile phone at school, only use it when necessary. When I first got my mobile phone, I was only allowed to use it in emergencies. Now that I'm older, I use it a lot more, but I don't use it excessively. Be whatever you want and do whatever you want, but there is always a consequence for what you do. With regard to mobile phones, if you abuse it (if you have one), not only will you get a huge bill, but your parents might take it away from you. Also, you may get into trouble if you use it during class, so I advise you to wait until out of class to use it. • Damian

★ I think Damian covered that topic well. Mobile phones are very handy and useful in emergencies and to stay in contact with your family and friends, but they can be bad when they are abused. You can become addicted to using your mobile phone. Also, the mobile phone can be a way for bullies to harass you. Ignore any text messages you receive that are abusive or inappropriate. If they don't stop, you can report it, and the person's number can be traced. And never give your phone number out unless you know the person well. • Josie

MOM – Female parent/guardian

Your mom is important to you. You may have fights with your mom, but in the end, your mom is still an important person. • Damian

Thanks, Damian … I think! Having a female role model in your life is important, whether that is your mother, grandmother, aunt or a female guardian. Having a connection with a female helps you with your future relationships with other females. You probably find that your mother plays a very important part in your life, as she helps and guides you. Sometimes it is hard to realize that some of the things she does or suggests are because she loves you and wants the best for you. Sometimes it's easier for you to be angry with the person closest to you, but it's unfair to take it out on your mother. • Josie

MONEY – A medium of exchange, for example, cash, coin, check, etc.

Money is basically like a trading tool. Money is nice! The best way to get money is to have a job or a career (see Job or Career). Gambling is also a way but not a good way. I personally never gamble because there is always a risk that I'll lose. I don't like risks. • Damian

Yes, money is a trading tool and is a necessity in our current lifestyle. If you learn how to budget your money, that will help you in the future. Learning to earn, budget, spend and save is the key to managing your money wisely. • Josie

MORALS – Ideals, customs, beliefs, principles and ethics

Morals are like rules you develop and adhere to personally for what to do and what not to do. It is a good idea to follow morals because they may stop you from doing things you might regret later. Morals are usually based on religious beliefs and traditions, rather than the law. For example, one of my morals is to never take advantage of another person. Why? Because I consider myself a good and decent person. • Damian

⭐ Morals are manners and customs that you personally choose to take on; as Damian said, they are not laws of society, but can be unspoken personal or even community laws. One person's morals can be different from another's; that's why sometimes we don't get along with people as they may have different morals from our own. That doesn't mean we should judge people for their morals, as they are an individual choice. For example, if you find a wallet in the street and it has one hundred dollars in it, you have several choices. The right thing to do morally is to hand it in as you found it. The immoral thing to do is to take the money out of the wallet and throw the wallet away. Not only is it illegal, as it would be stealing; it is also an immoral choice. • Josie

MUSIC – Vocal/instrumental sounds/tones resulting in melodies, harmony or rhythm

🌀 Music! I love certain types of music; other types I hate. Everyone has his or her personal taste, which usually depends on the person's personality or culture. It's like a class thing that teenagers use to categorize themselves for some reason. Don't use music to judge your friends. • Damian

⭐ Music is a great way to express yourself, either by listening to it, dancing to it, playing an instrument or writing songs. You may have talent in an area of music. Damian is a great pianist and has a remarkable ear for music; he can hear a song and then play the notes on the piano without a music sheet. • Josie

NAME CALLING – Insulting and abusing labels

Name-calling is a stupid thing that people like to do, either to bully someone they don't like or to annoy a friend as a joke. People at my school name-call, just like they do at nearly every school. Some of my friends call each other "idiot" and stuff, but it is really not a good thing. Sometimes name-calling can lead to bullying (see Bullying). • Damian

Name-calling is a verbal form of bullying. It is a verbal insult. Some-times friends joke with each other and call each other names. This is only okay if both get the joke. To be able to tell if it's a joke or not, listen to the tone in which the word is said. If it is said in a light, joking way, then it is probably a joke. If it is said in a harsh and sneering way, it is an insult. You may learn how to tell the difference between jokes or non-jokes from social understanding/skills classes, or if you have a friend who doesn't have Asperg-er, ask for some help in being a "joke detective." If you are a victim of con-stant name-calling, take action to have it stopped – such as walking away, asking the person to stop, or telling an adult about the situation. • Josie

NORMAL – Ordinary, usual, standard, regular, typical and common

Normal? This is a pretty stupid subject, because, really, nobody is nor-mal. Some people use "normal" as another word for "average." Is it a good thing to be average? To not be unique? I don't think so. Think of this: Why do people want to buy unique items from stores? Why are collectibles with a spelling mistake or misprint worth MUCH more than the "normal" collect-ibles? Because they're not normal! They're unique! • Damian

"Normal" basically means standard, ordinary, usual and typical. The word "normal" gets used a lot around a diagnosis. Personally, I am not a standard, ordinary, usual or typical person; therefore, I am not normal by the standard definition. People with AS are not standard, ordinary, usual or typical; therefore, you are unique. So I think we should celebrate non-normalness! Nevertheless, if you are really trying to feel "normal," that's okay, too. But don't stress out about it. Be who you are. • Josie

OBSESSIONS – Fixations, infatuations, compulsions or severe fascinations

Obsessions are thoughts, behaviors or activities that you keep thinking, talking about or doing all the time. If, for example, you love a show on TV and you're always thinking about it without thinking about anything else, then you're obsessed with that show. I used to have sooo many obsessions! Pokémon, computers, Batman. Why not have obsessions? Because (a) if that's all you talk about or do, people will find you boring; and (b) if your obsessions are the only way to fully be happy, then what happens when the obsessions disappear? • Damian

Obsessiveness can involve an object or a person. It's a behavior whereby you think and talk about something/someone constantly, to the point that it dominates your life. The thought or sight of your obsession brings you good feelings – nothing else brings you the same good feelings. That's why you become obsessed with that object/person because you want those feelings to keep happening.

People with AS are prone to obsessive behaviors, possibly as a way of feeling secure and safe. Sometimes obsessions can come in handy; in particular, if you know a lot about something/somebody, it also makes you an expert. It is important to emphasize the difference between obsessions and special interests. Having a special interest is O.K. As you become very knowledgeable about the topic, it becomes your hobby and brings you a lot of joy. But if your special interest begins to take over all your waking hours, and if you start to feel anxious when you don't get to spend time on your interest, then it is becoming an obsession. It's all about finding a balance. If you prefer to think of things in a mathematical way, let's use percentages as an example. If you are thinking/ talking about your obsession more than 30 percent of the waking hours of a day, then it is unhealthy for you, and possibly others. If you need help to deal with obsessive behaviors, talk to a counselor or psychologist, as he or she can show you some strategies and help you gain balance in your life. • Josie

ODORS – A pleasant or unpleasant smell

An odor is a smell. Bad smells can come from a person and be called B.O. (body odor). If you worry about having B.O., wash and shower and use deodorant. In sixth grade I kept forgetting to use deodorant (because I had just started to use it), and people used to comment on my smell. I wasn't very happy with the people for commenting, but I could have solved the problem by writing a note to remind myself to put some deodorant on. I didn't think of that at the time, but as I got older, I eventually got used to washing and showering more and putting deodorant on every day. • Damian

Sometimes we can't smell our own body odor, but others can. Bad body odor can result from a lack of cleanliness. To be sure that you don't have bad body odor, it's important to be hygienic and clean by bathing/showering regularly, and that includes washing your hair with shampoo. Also brush your teeth twice a day, wear clean clothes and put on deodorant. Don't panic – if you are unsure as to whether you smell bad – ask somebody you trust. • Josie

ORGANIZED – Be orderly, structured, prepared and planned

If you're organized, you'll never miss important dates and everything you do is well planned, and that's really great! I am generally organized, but when it comes to keeping a record of dates and homework, that's when I go down-hill; something I have to work on. It's good to have a planner for all that stuff, because everything you need to know is in this one little book or computer that's always with you. Totally forgot when that major assignment is due? Check your planner. Easy! • Damian

I have been trying to get Damian to keep a planner for years. Just as adults have planners to keep track of their appointments, special days, and so on, it's important for you to start this habit. Being organized comes in especially handy in your senior years of schooling, at university and work, and even in your relationships. With modern technology, you are very lucky – you don't need to use a paper planner, you can use an on-line calendar, the calendar in your mobile phone, your computer, and so on. Being organized will help you feel better about your life, and you will be more confident in what your day has ahead of you. We used lots of schedules and charts for Damian in his elementary years; these worked well – he would check to see what was on the next day and plan for it. Now that he has to do it himself, he doesn't always do it, unfortunately. One final comment about organization and schedules: No matter how well you plan and how organized you try to be, change will happen. Keep that in mind, so you don't get totally overwhelmed if your schedule changes. • Josie

OUTCAST – A person or thing rejected by society

An outcast is someone who has basically been excluded and is never in-cluded in any groups. I used to be an outcast with only one friend, but I didn't care because we'd have our own fun and didn't really notice that there were other groups. If you notice someone is being excluded, it would be good of you to try to include them in whatever you're doing. • Damian

Society has a habit of casting out people who don't fit in or conform. I be-lieve this is discrimination. It is common in schools for groups of children to cast out the odd or different student, only because they don't understand them – not because there is anything wrong with them. If you feel you are being ignored or excluded, speak up, talk to an adult about it, and find out why it is happening and how it can be changed unless, of course, you prefer it that way. • Josie

PARENTS – Your origins: mother, father or guardians

Parents (even if I hate to admit it!) usually know what they're talking about. It is a good idea to listen to them. Sure, you might think their ways are old and unreasonable. When I was little, my mom used to make me do jobs; I thought it was because she didn't want me to have fun, etc. But now that I look back, she had a reason to make me do those things; she did it to make me independent so that as an adult, I can move out and do everything my way! • Damian

When Damian was first diagnosed 12 years ago, I was told by the doctor that he would never marry and would live at home forever … (as mentioned earlier, not much was understood about Asperger Syndrome back then). I didn't want that to happen; I wanted him to be independent.

Yay, Damian plans to move out! Success! Of course, as in so many other instances, what works for one person, in this case, Damian, may not be appropriate or work equally well for somebody else. So, if you are not ready to move out, don't feel bad about yourself. • Josie

PARTIES – Social gatherings of people celebrating a specific occasion

Parties, I love them (I'm talking about random teenage parties). I love the social stuff. This is probably an area where I am different from most teenagers with Asperger Syndrome, who may find social situations overwhelming and not like parties at all. If you do go to one of these types of parties, here's my advice: Don't drink or try drugs, and don't smoke anything. There are other ways to have fun, such as just talking to people, watching a movie and playing games. • Damian

There are lots of different types of parties. The kind Damian is talking about is the typical teenage party. There are other parties such as a celebration or a family party. If you are invited to a party, remember, to be safe, do everything in moderation. Parents can become very paranoid about these types of parties, so listen to their advice. If you feel uncomfortable at a party, don't hesitate to call your parents to be picked up early. As a teenager with Asperger Syndrome, you may not even be attracted to any party because it seems unpleasant or too much hard work to be social. This is O.K. Some teens with Asperger's think they have to fit in and can get themselves into situations they don't like or that get them into trouble. Remember to do what you want, not what others want you to do. • Josie

PEERS – People of the same generation, rank, ability – your equals

Peers? This is like classmates and other kids your own age. Respect your classmates, in general. Of course, if they are mean and they bully you, they don't deserve any respect. Try not to idolize a classmate, because if you do and you start acting like this person and agreeing to everything he or she does, people will pick up on it and then may bully you about that. • Damian

Yes, Damian, peers are people of your own generation or your equals. The term "peer pressure" is about how you can be heavily influenced by people your own age. Sometimes, this is pretty harmless; for example, if you try to dress like the coolest group in school because you want people to think you are cool. In other instances, peer pressure may lead young people to try smoking, drinking, drugs, etc. That's when it gets bad. • Josie

PERSONAL SAFETY – Individual protection or security

Don't be naive about safety. Don't do stupid things just to be cool. Think logically about what you're going to do before you do something. Also, don't be aggressive towards people because you might get yourself into some serious trouble. It can provoke people into becoming violent towards you. • Damian

Personal safety has to do with protecting yourself; in particular, planning ahead. For example, if you're going home late from work or school, and you know it's going to be dark, plan ahead by organizing a ride or something. Another example is if you are going to a party, make sure you are with somebody you know and trust, so if anything happens to you, you have help at hand. Personal safety is also about having safe sex. • Josie

POLICE – A governmental force keeping order, preventing crime and enforcing the law

Police! When I was in elementary school, I was afraid of the police because I thought they could arrest you for no reason, just because they felt like it. Obviously, this isn't true. If you are stopped by the police and asked questions, DO NOT LIE! Once I lied to the police and got into a lot of trouble. So yeah, don't repeat my mistake! • Damian

Police officers are law enforcers; exactly that. Their job is to maintain law and order in society. If you break the law, you may become involved with the police. As Damian said, do not lie, as this is a crime in itself. There are many incidents where teenagers with Asperger Syndrome have unfortunate encounters with the police. In one case, a teen with AS hung around a group that accepted him, but they weren't positive role models; they were into drug taking and drug dealing. The guy with AS didn't take or deal drugs but just hung out with them because they were his "friends," or so he thought. But, in reality, they were using him as a scapegoat. One night the police turned up where they were hanging out, and they threw the bag of drugs at the teen with AS and all quickly disappeared. So the teen with AS was taken down to the station and charged with possession of drugs, and the others got away. If you have certain behaviors or characteristics due to your Asperger Syndrome, you may draw attention to yourself, and some police officers don't understand Asperger Syndrome and its characteristics. If you are apprehended or approached by the police, it is a good idea to identify that you have Asperger Syndrome. It does not mean the label gives you an excuse for illegal acts, but it can help you out with the way in which things are communicated. • Josie

POPULARITY – Widespread acceptance

Popularity … gee … this is one of my least favorite topics. My search for popularity early in high school was very tiresome and frustrating, and when I look back now, I see it was unnecessary. Usually during school, popularity is very important to students. My advice, don't do anything stupid in hopes of becoming popular, such as doing crazy stunts or breaking rules. Just be yourself and don't worry too much about what others think. Be kind and considerate (see also Peer Pressure). • Damian

I'm going to give you an example of positive popularity. Damian's sister is very popular, and she's not a bimbo or a try-hard or wannabe (someone who tries so hard to fit in). She is very kind, nice, smart and accepts everybody; she isn't nasty and doesn't gossip or judge people. This is why she is popular. And the good thing is, she doesn't try to be popular. She just is naturally popular. But not everyone is naturally popular like she is, and that's OK. Not everyone will like you. That's normal, just like you may not like everyone. • Josie

PROBLEM-SOLVING – Working or figuring out a difficulty

Problem-solving, the name explains itself. When it comes to problem-solving, try solving issues a bit like a math equation. Write down all the information you have, and then write down how you are going to solve it, including the pros and cons. • Damian

Very good, Damian. Yes you can either problem solve by writing the issue down and solving it like a mathematical equation, or you can talk to somebody and get some advice. To be able to problem solve is very important – especially as you get older, as situations in life become more challenging. • Josie

PUNISHMENT – Discipline or penalty for a wrong act

Punishment is like consequences. If you do something bad, something bad will happen to you. Usually this is done by the law (you commit a crime, you go to jail or get fined) or by society (you do something bad even if it isn't illegal, and people may ignore you or be rude to you). So be nice. • Damian

Very simply, every action has a consequence. Nice action = nice consequence. Bad action = bad consequence. • Josie

QUESTION – An inquiry or asking when you are uncertain, to resolve or learn

Unfortunately, I have a habit of asking too many questions, often at times when people are busy or stressed. My mom sometimes ignores me, and this REALLY irritates me. All she needs to say is "I can't think right now,

Damian" nicely, instead of not saying anything; that's just rude! In class you can usually ask questions, but sometimes when you ask too many questions, teachers may say, "Well, you should know that already," and then not answer your question. If this happens say, "I'm sorry; I don't know it; could you please help me or tell me how to find out?" Teachers are there to teach you, not ignore you. • Damian

Yes, Damian does ask a lot of questions; sometimes he asks a question more than once, and sometimes he asks questions that he already knows the answer to! I do not ignore him; it's just that sometimes he asks when I am very busy and concentrating on something else, so I don't hear him. Also when I do say, "I can't think right now" or "I am busy," Damian takes it personally and gets angry with me. I suggest if you have a multitude of questions and it's not the right time to ask somebody, write them down (as I have suggested to Damian at times) so you don't forget them. Then you can ask the person when it is a good time to sit down with him/her and have your questions answered. • Josie

QUIET TIME – A peaceful and tranquil moment

Quiet time is good for relaxing and calming down. When you're angry, upset or stressed, it is often a good idea to go to your room or somewhere nice and quiet where you can just relax. Whenever I feel anxious, I go to my room for a little while. I don't do anything, maybe just sit down and run some thoughts through my head. Sometimes I listen to music. • Damian

Quiet time is great for exactly the reasons Damian gave. When Damian was in elementary school, he used to have quiet time at school and was allowed to sit away from the class in a beanbag chair to chill out for five minutes. This gave him time to wind down and gain some energy for the rest of the day. A lot of people with AS need quiet time to release and process all the input from the day. Quiet time when you get home from school is also very important. Sometimes, if Damian comes home in a bad mood and grunts at me, I grunt back, I don't even talk to him – just give him a snack and he goes off to his room to watch a DVD. In this way he has quiet time; he winds down, the DVD distracts his mind from the day, the time on his own de-stresses him, and when he emerges from his room later on, we then have a conversation about the day. • Josie

REBELLIOUS – Rioting, resisting authority or defiant type of behavior

🌀 I don't like it when people are being rebellious for no reason. A lot of teen-agers act that way to their parents, teachers, and even sometimes their friends, for absolutely no reason (or no good reason anyway). But that's just how they are, and they have that right. My advice about rebellion: Have a good reason to rebel because if you don't, no one will take you seriously. • Damian

★ Actually, people have a reason: Even if they don't understand the reason why they are rebelling, it's because of an unsettled, restless or angry feeling they have inside that they can't seem to work out. A lot of teenagers are rebellious because they are resisting authority – they want to make their own decisions and don't want their life to be dictated to them. It's a normal stage of the teen years to feel a little rebellious. It's O.K. to have an opinion, but you don't need to force other people to listen to or understand your opinion. If you are rebelling, and it is causing other people difficulties or discomfort, it can become a problem. At times, adolescents with Asperger Syndrome need more support than others their age because of choices they are unable to make, so you may feel unfairly treated, but in fact your guardians/parents are protecting you. • Josie

RELATIVES – Family members connected to you by blood or marriage

Relatives are awesome (mine anyway). They are the ones that will always be there for you. They are like your supreme friends. Always try to show respect. I know it can be really annoying when your older relatives say "show some respect," but it means a lot to them. • Damian

Gee thanks, Damian, we're "awesome!" Relatives are the people who are in your family tree. There are some relatives who are our favorites and then there are some relatives with whom we may not get along. That's okay, because everyone has a personality, and personalities can clash sometimes. But as Damian says, it's nice to respect your family – even the ones you don't get along with. If nothing else, try to stay away and mind your own business. • Josie

RELAXATION – A rest time from work, school or stress in your life

Relaxation is excellent. I love to just lie or sit down after a long day and have something to eat or drink in front of the TV. It's a wind-down. Relaxation not only feels good, it's good for your health. You can also get wonderful relaxation by meditating (see Meditation). • Damian

Relaxation is a very important part of the day. You can relax by either doing what Damian does, by having a hobby, or through physical exercise. Do whatever it is that makes your muscles relax, makes your eyes relax and makes you give a big sigh – releasing all that pent-up energy. • Josie

RESPONSIBLE – Being accountable for your behavior

Responsibilities are very important. Never take a responsibility as a joke. It is what prepares you for a successful and responsible future as an adult. For example, my mom made my sister and me independent by giving us responsibilities when we were young and gradually giving us more and more as we grew up. Responsibilities can be as small as cleaning your room or feeding your pet, but no matter how small, they're important, and if you don't follow them, there are usually negative consequences. For example, Pet + No Food = Death of Pet from starvation. Did you like my math? • Damian

I don't think I need to add anything else; explained very well. • Josie

REVENGE – The act of retaliation – returning an insult/injury to someone

Hmmmmm … Revenge … Well yes, I could go on about how revenge is bad and how you shouldn't do it, but then I'd be a hypocrite. Though many people have told me that revenge is stupid, I happen to be a big fan of revenge. I see it as justice, but that's just my opinion. • Damian

Hmm, I totally disagree with Damian, but then that knowledge has probably come with age, because when I was younger, I would've thought the same as Damian regarding revenge. Now as an adult, I realize that if you seek revenge on someone, then you are just as bad as the person you are getting back it. Also, by holding a grudge or getting revenge, you are in a way giving away your "power" – it's like having an invisible cord connected to that person. If you can move on from the situation, you have your own power back, and that invisible cord has been cut. • Josie

RULES – Required dos and don'ts, conduct, methods and procedures

Rules are necessary, whether we like them or not. When you're younger, usually you don't understand why rules are made and why we have to follow them. Rules help stop you from being selfish, harming yourself and others, doing illegal things, etc. When I was younger, I didn't understand why my parents had to boss me around so much, but I eventually did. What I don't understand is why they keep doing it today. • Damian

You think we are bossing you around, but it's only because we love you, Damian. Many persons with Asperger Syndrome thrive on rules and predictability. Often, they are referred to as the "rule police" as they have a tendency to dictate rules to others (e.g., you may see somebody wearing the wrong uniform at school and you tell them so or tell a teacher). • Josie

RUMOR – Gossip, scandal, an unsubstantiated story

Never assume rumors to be true and never start and participate in rumors. It's like that game "Chinese Whispers" or "Telephone." Everyone sits in a circle and someone starts a phrase and whispers it to someone else, and then they whisper it to the next person, and so on, until it comes back to the original person and you compare how much it has changed. Rumors work similar to that: People change it all the time, even without knowing it. Sometimes people make up stories – rumors – to give someone else a bad reputation. That's happened many times at my school. Not to me but to others (see also Gossip). • Damian

Rumors are plain and simple unconfirmed stories – a little like gossip. It is rude and bad manners to start rumors; in fact, it is a form of harassment. It is also rude to spread rumors after you have been told a rumor. So if somebody comes to you with a rumor about somebody, just nod, smile, say nothing and let it stop there – don't pass it on to anybody else. If you are the victim of rumors/stories that are untrue, it can be very sad and frustrating. While it is tempting to reason that you know what the truth is and if people choose to believe otherwise why would you be interested in their approval or how they think of you. However, sometimes it is necessary to take action to protect yourself against rumors that may be a form of harassment. So if you are unsure whether a rumor is actually harassment, talk to an adult about it. • Josie

RUNAWAY – A person who has run away from home or school

A runaway is someone who has run away from home. Running away from home is a very serious act and can result in great harm. If you have a problem at home, it can be tempting to threaten to leave but DON'T. Really, where would you go? Also, you cannot run away from things. It is much better to try to deal with whatever it is that's bothering you. Sure, I've been really pissed off with my parents and my sister at certain times, and I just feel like leaving, but I know that it's not responsible to do so. • Damian

Even when you are very upset and want to "get away from everybody," it is not necessary to physically run away. Discuss your feelings with somebody or write them down in a journal. When appropriate, talk to friends or a trusted adult. You can get away from your problems, at least for a while, by having quiet time or taking some time away in your room, spending time with a pet or doing some physical exercise. Or if the problems are at school, you can go to a safe place like the library or whatever arrangements you may have with your teachers. • Josie

SAD – An emotion that makes you feel unhappy, gloomy, depressed

No matter how well you think things are going, life has its sad times. There is no way you can be happy all the time. There will be times when a family member dies, a pet dies, a friend abandons you, or your girlfriend/boyfriend leaves you. You can get sad over even smaller things. When you do get sad, let it out as quickly as you can. Cry if you must; who cares about what others will think if they see you cry. I've never cried in front of others, not because of what they think of me, but because I like to keep my negative feelings as private as I can. But that's just me. • Damian

Sadness is an emotion. It's not necessarily a negative one, but it is an important one that everyone is likely to feel at one point or another, as Damian wrote. As Damian said, if you feel sad, try to feel it, and then move on from the feeling. If you don't express it, or try to block it, the feeling becomes suppressed. That is not healthy, as it can build up and affect you and your relationships, both now and later in life. It's okay to feel sad about both small or big incidents in your life. If you are feeling sad for no reason, this can be okay too – your hormones can play a part in this. If you are feeling sad all the time and don't know why, then it's best to talk to a parent or your doctor as there may be a chemical imbalance happening in your body. • Josie

SARCASM – A sneering, jeering, taunting or ridiculing remark

Sarcasm is hard to describe. It's basically when someone purposely says the opposite of what they mean and tries to make it known by voice, body language, etc. For example, someone says to me "are you female?" I'll say sarcastically, "yes ... I'm female, can't you tell?" and my tone of voice will imply that the question was stupid. Back when I was younger, I used to fall for sarcasm and couldn't tell if someone was being sarcastic. Even today I still sometimes fail to understand when someone is being sarcastic. • Damian

That's okay, Damian. I too fail sometimes to notice if somebody is sarcastic! People with AS have difficulty interpreting sarcasm. But Damian is right, you can usually tell by the tone of voice used, because the person using sarcasm is purposely exaggerating. If you are not sure whether somebody is telling the truth or being sarcastic, ask or ignore it. • Josie

SCHOOL – A teaching and learning institution

For some, school can be the best part of life; for others, the worst. I don't particularly like school, doing work isn't much fun and sometimes lunch can get really boring. Besides, some people get bullied (which really upsets me). I personally don't get bullied now because I've made myself fit in, and the students have matured out of bullying. In elementary school it was pretty bad, and it usually resulted in fistfights because kids would provoke me. If you don't enjoy school because of the students, hopefully you will be happier later in life when you have more choices about whom you spend time with, so don't get too upset – the rest of your life will not necessarily be like that. If you don't enjoy school because of the work, well, your happiness might come after school if you find a job you like. • Damian

 School is an essential part of your life as a teenager. If you take away the social side of it, you are there to learn and absorb information that will prepare you for your future. Yes, unfortunately the downside of school for some is the anti-social behaviors, bullying and workload that school can represent. If you just can't stand school and do not cope well with going there – there are other options. To find out these options, discuss your feelings about school with either your parents or a school counselor. Damian was home-schooled part time at one stage to give him a break from the stresses of elementary school; he loved home-schooling so much it was hard to get him to go back to school full time. However, we decided it was best for him to go back, so he

could interact with others on a social basis. Today, we discussed whether this was a wise choice as school has not been something Damian has enjoyed. We both agreed that if he had been home-schooled for the rest of his school career, he would never have been able to form the friendship circle he has worked so hard to attain. • Josie

SELF-ESTEEM – Positive belief and pride in oneself

Your self-esteem is very important. If you don't like yourself, you're not going to be happy. I used to have really bad self-esteem, so bad that I remember being in the car and wishing another car would smash into us so that I'd die. It got a lot worse just recently, to the point where I hated myself so much I was about to give up on life. I eventually got over it, though, and raised my self-esteem by minimizing the things I hated about myself (bad childhood due to bullying, being different, etc.) and expressing the things I loved about myself (i.e., being smart). • Damian

Gee thanks, Damian, I hope I wasn't in that car that you wished crashed! Self-esteem is something you have to build through your belief system. If you believe that you are unworthy or worthless, you have low self-esteem. But if you believe that you are an important and special person who deserves the best, you have good self-esteem. You can get some help with raising your self-esteem through counseling, social skills activities, and so on. If you begin to make even a few, smaller achievements – not just academic, but in other areas of your life where you set goals and work toward them – this is a positive thing and adds to your self-esteem. Life is often like a set of scales, up and down, up and down, but if the scale stays down more than up, ask for help – it's not a nice place to stay in all the time • Josie

SECRETS – Information kept hidden from others

 Secrets are sacred. If someone tells you DO NOT TELL ANYONE ELSE – unless, of course, it affects your own or their safety – the best advice is not to tell. Earning people's trust is important. If people can trust you, they'll respect you. In 10th grade I was the secret guru. Everyone would tell me his or her secrets, because they knew I wouldn't tell anyone. It can be hard to find somebody who will keep your secret. If you have a secret and you want to get it off your back, tell a close friend or a relative. Only really close friends are trustworthy. Others may tell you that they will keep your secret only to use it against you by telling it after all. • Damian

 Not much more for me to say. I believe that people with AS are very good at keeping other people's secrets, because if you are asked not to tell anybody … then you don't! It's as easy as that. But as Damian said, if you are told a secret where somebody is in an unsafe situation, then it is O.K., even essential, to tell. • Josie

SENSORY OVERLOAD – Too great a load placed on the body's neurological receptors and transmitters

 I haven't had a sensory overload for years. But I remember experiencing it. Once in fifth grade when everyone in the class was really loud, I couldn't take it. I just lay on my desk with my hands covering my eyes and attempted to cover my ears with my arms. Sensory overloads can occur from any of the five senses, sight, hearing, smell, taste and touch. Being in a crowd and being touched by a lot of people can lead to sensory overload. If you get sensory overload, either do what I used to do or try to escape the area that is too much for you. If this is a classroom, maybe ask the teacher if you could have a 5-minute break (or maybe even just ask if you could go to the toilet). • Damian

★ Exactly, sensory overload means that your senses (sight, hearing, touch, etc.) have absorbed way too much information. Your body can't cope anymore, and you feel like you need to explode or shut down. For many people with AS, sensory overload can happen at school, at a noisy and crowded restaurant or in crowded public transportation. If you teach yourself some strategies on how to cope in these situations, then it will help you deal with overload. For example, if you have auditory challenges, you can wear earplugs or headphones. • Josie

SHADOWING – To secretly follow or stay close to a person without his or her knowledge

This is like stalking (see Stalking), only the person you're shadowing doesn't know you're doing it. You might follow from a distance or watch the person's house from afar with a telescope or something without the victim knowing. My advice? Don't do it. It is illegal, and people find it freaky and won't like you for it. • Damian

★ Yes, it is illegal to shadow someone unless you are a private investigator. Unfortunately, you may not even know you are shadowing somebody. For example, you might really like somebody and be fascinated by her (or him) and want to know all about her, where she lives, what she does; maybe you need to see her all the time without her knowing – this is shadowing. If you are in this situation, you may have become obsessed with that person (see Obsessions). If you are the victim of somebody stalking or shadowing you, report it to your school, family or the police. • Josie

SHAVING – Cutting or scraping hair away from the body

I started shaving when I was 13 years old. When you're younger and you are waiting to shave, you're like "ohh!! I can't wait till I have to shave!!!" Trust me, that'll wear off soon after you start. Once you have to do it all the time, it becomes annoying. I use an electric shaver because my dad uses one. You can use whatever type of shaver you want, but you'll probably use the one your Dad or guardian uses because they will be the one to teach you how to shave. • Damian

Damian is the expert here; he has more experience in the matter of facial hair! • Josie

SIBLING – brother, half brother, half sister, kinsman, offspring, sister

Your siblings can get VERY annoying. You'll have fights and sometimes hate each other, but they are always your siblings. If you try to get along, then you can have a supportive person there for you. My sister and I used to fight all the time, we never talked about anything, and I'd always be very angry with her. One day I decided to make the effort to be nice and see what would happen. Now we get along really well, and we can talk to each other about issues that bother us. • Damian

You are a sibling to your brother or sister, and they are siblings to you. A sibling is a blood-related brother or sister. Damian and his sister Chiara are siblings. Sometimes siblings do not get along because they live under the same roof day in and day out, and sometimes there is jealousy if they feel one or the other are being favored by parents, just like Damian and Chiara! Damian thinks his father favors Chiara, and Chiara thinks I favor Damian. As siblings grow up, their relationships with each other and their parents change and mature, and usually it gets easier for everybody to get along. Now that my kids get on better with each other, they gang up on me. On a serious note, it can be difficult for siblings to have a brother with Asperger's; they have opinions and emotions about your diagnosis as well as you do. • Josie

SLEEPLESS – Unable to sleep – feeling restless at night

I've had many nights with barely any sleep for apparently no reason. I can never understand it. My eyes will get so heavy they hurt, yet I still can't get to sleep. And when you get irritated because you want to go to sleep, it only makes matters worse. What do I do? Try sprinkling lavender oil on your pillow or try anything that relieves stress, such as listening to music, taking a hot bath, etc. In an Asperger conference recently, I learned that lack of sleep is a major issue for people with Asperger's. I found this very interesting. • Damian

If people have trouble sleeping, there is usually an underlying reason for it; you experience stress at work/school, you are having too much caffeine, or your mind is very busy. If you suffer from sleepless nights, try some relaxation strategies like lavender oil or meditation music. Exercising can also help as your muscles become tired, or you can try taking a warm bath. We were on holiday last year and there was one night where I had to share a room with Damian. We turned the light out to sleep, and he whined and whined about not being able to sleep, but I knew he was overtired. I couldn't stand it any longer, so I sprinkled lavender oil over his pillow and gave him my eye mask; he was off in sleep land within minutes! When I have trouble sleeping, instead of lying there tossing and turning, I get up, make myself a cup of tea and a piece of toast and watch television, and within an hour I am back to bed fast asleep. Individuals with AS may have rough sleep patterns or may even have issues with sleeping because of their medication. If you have chronic trouble sleeping and can't seem to pinpoint the cause, talk to your doctor about it. • Josie

SLEEPOVER – Spending a night at a place other than your own

I didn't go to many sleepovers when I was younger because I wasn't very popular, but the ones I did go to were usually fun. Remember that if you stay at a friend's house, you are the guest. You should follow the rules and be polite and nice to the parents because they're the ones who let you stay over. • Damian

Choosing to go to a sleepover is a personal thing. You may not like sleepovers because you prefer your own bed, or you may become curious and adventurous and want to experience somebody else's house. When my daughter Chiara had a sleepover birthday party a few years ago, when she was about 10, one of her guests was a young girl with AS, so we knew she might have special needs, especially in terms of sensory overload (see Sensory Overload). Chiara roped off a little section of the family room and posted a sign saying "ELEANOR'S TIME-AWAY PLACE." When Eleanor arrived, Chiara showed her the area and told her that if she felt like getting away, or if the party was too much for her, this was a special area that she could go to. Eleanor used the area a few times that night, as it was her very first sleepover and she had a mix of excitement and anxiety. This strategy worked very well. Maybe you are a little too old to rope areas off, but there are other strategies. Perhaps you could go outside for a breather, or if you really can't stand to be there any longer, ask to go home; it's absolutely your choice. • Josie

SOCIALIZING – To take an active part in a social (recreational) activity

Most people with AS don't like to socialize, but some do. I'm a bit in between. Sure, I love to socialize but only to a certain extent, and I always need a cooldown time where I can relax afterwards. At most, I like to socialize one day, maybe go out with friends, then relax and do nothing the

next few days. Sometimes people do not understand why you don't want to socialize. For example, at lunchtime if I want some quiet time, I go sit by myself. Sometimes some of my friends follow me and I'll be like, "hmmm great... not!" and think to myself, "Can you please go away?" But they want to socialize. If worse comes to worst, try and hide or just tell your friends you need some "alone time." • Damian

Socializing can be a difficult for people with AS because it involves social chitchat, which you may find awkward or meaningless. Finding the balance is the key; try to attend a few social events so you can practice your social skills. Some social events are a nightmare for people with AS, such as big, noisy parties with too many people in one area. But there are other social occasions, like a quiet dinner party, bowling, a club meeting, and so on, that may suit you more. Damian says he loves to socialize, but I know that if he has been socializing too much, when he comes home, he needs a lot of space from people to wind down and gather himself. • Josie

SOCIAL OCCASIONS – Recreational events

You may not like going to social occasions, and if that is the case, that's fine. Unfortunately for you, there will be times when you'll have to go to them. It will just be one of those things in life you won't be happy about. Don't get too stressed out about them because if you're struggling to get through them, just think that tomorrow you'll not be in a social occasion and that all you have to do is make it through the night. When I was younger, I didn't like them at all, and this was what I thought to myself to get through it. • Damian

I believe that Damian has taught himself to shut a lot of stimuli out when he is at a social occasion, and therefore he enjoys them now. The school dance (or prom) can be very stressful for someone with AS. What do I wear? Who do I bring? How do I dance? Of course, you have the choice not to attend. If you want to attend, prepare yourself beforehand (like the camp preparations; see Summer Camp). In this way you will be feeling safer and less stressed for the occasion. • Josie

SOCIAL SKILLS – Being able to take part in entertaining group activities. Techniques used when interacting with others

Oh, my ... social skills! Those are one of the main problems those of us with AS have – ha-ha! Well, basically, this includes stuff like eye contact, how to address people, what is expected in certain situations and all the other social stuff we don't like. Thing is, to live successfully in this world, unfortunately, we have to learn, or at least make an effort to learn, these things. The world is not as kind and as accepting as we'd like to think, and people aren't going to excuse us just because we have AS. Social skills can be learned in social skills classes. I started going to them when I was 5, and they really helped me. • Damian

Social skills are important to learn if you want to fit into society. This is true not just for people with AS but for everybody. Some people have natural social skills; they seem to instinctively know what to do or say in a social situation. Others need to be taught or guided. Damian has learned social skills to the extent that he may not necessarily know why he is doing something, but he knows that is the way it is expected. For example, with regard to eye contact, Damian does not like looking at another person's eyes, but knows that people without Asperger Syndrome like to have eye contact when they are speaking or being spoken to. Damian does not expect the other person to give him eye contact. Think of it like a computer game: There are certain skills you need to demonstrate to be able to play it. You may have a talent at knowing the skills, or you may have to learn them, but either way, you need them to play the game. Socializing is like playing a game whereby people take turns to talk, and so on. • Josie

SPECIAL EDUCATION – Specific education program for students who need alternative teaching approaches

Special education can be in a separate school, but mostly it refers to special classes or assistance provided for students who need special help in certain areas. When I was 8, I went to a special education school, and they helped me learn how to live in the community by teaching me social skills and other subjects I had difficulty with. In high school, there was a special education department in our school. This was really great because whenever I needed help or even just to get away for a little while, I could go there. • Damian

There are times when you may need special services; for Damian, these times were usually when he was highly stressed or needed time away. There were also times when Damian rejected special education because he didn't want to appear different or be bullied about it. Now Damian is an active part of his education plan and attends all meetings with us so he is aware of what is happening for him. He also contributes to the meetings by stating his needs or what he doesn't need. The special education staff at his school in the past few years have concentrated more on his abilities than his disabilities. They have helped him with his career plans. For example, they arranged his work experience in a medical laboratory, which then offered him a one-day-a-week traineeship, which helped Damian's entry into college to study science. • Josie

STALKING – Pursue, hunt and follow another person in a harassing, obsessive way

Stalking is the extreme of shadowing (see Shadowing). It's when you follow someone and watch them all the time. If you do or are tempted to do this, don't. Try to get over the person you are stalking by finding out why you are stalking them; once you've discovered the reason, usually you stop, because discovering reasons can be all that you need to solve the problem. If you're the victim, tell someone and get help. • Damian

S Yes, stalking means pestering an individual when he or she basically doesn't want to know you. Stalking can consist of persistent shadowing, following, telephoning or approaching somebody, especially if the person has shown that he or she is not interested in having a friendship or relationship with you. On the other side, like Damian said, if you are the victim of stalking, report it, so the stalker can stop and get help as well. • Josie

STRATEGIES – Procedures, tactics and plans

Strategies are tools you can use to organize your life or perform certain tasks. I was lucky that my mom made me schedules, charts and checklists to help me in my life. For example, in elementary school, my mom made me a checklist of things to do in the morning to get ready for school. Using tools like this, you can make a routine of your day that makes it more efficient and much less stressful. • Damian

 I am a great believer in strategies. I am a very organized person, but to be organized I need plans, my journal, a routine, lists, and so on. Otherwise, because I am very busy, my life would be chaos, and I would become stressed. I recommend you plan your days and weeks by using a schedule, planner, organizer or journal. Also, if you have a project due or a busy day ahead, make a list of what you need to achieve and mark things off as you go. Having that list in front of you is like having a seatbelt on; you feel more in control and much safer. • Josie

STRESS – Mental tension, strain and pressure

I used to get terribly stressed in class when I was in elementary school. I can't even remember why I got so stressed, but I did. I used to rip the pages of my book, cover my ears and rest my head on the desk to block out noise (see Sensory Overload). I even used to throw my desk around. I found that playing the piano calmed me down, so whenever I got stressed, I would be excused by the teacher to go to the piano room to unwind. If you get stressed at your school, try to see if you can organize something like this. Try never to release your stress on others by yelling, hitting, etc. • Damian

Sometimes, if Damian is highly stressed and I badger him a little, I become the scapegoat (victim) of Damian's stress attack. Stress is a build-up of mental or physical tension. You can feel stress in your body, your heart beats faster, your breathing is faster, your muscles tighten and you may grit your teeth. If you allow your stress levels to build up, you will become like a volcano, and will eventually blow your top. But if you occasionally release your stress in stages before it builds up, you will not reach such a high stress level. It's like having a glass with water constantly dripping in it (the water is the stress, the glass is your body). If the glass gets full to the top, even a single drop will eventually cause it to spill over (this is the explosion), but if you have a small hole in the bottom of the glass, this releases the water gradually (releasing stress). There are various ways of de-stressing, such as relaxing by watching a favorite program, going for a swim, meditating, listening to music, having a massage, learning breathing techniques or taking a bath. The ultimate aim of stress releasers is to lower your blood pressure and slow down your heart rate. • Josie

STUDY – Research, memorize, learn, read, examine and reflect

Study is good, but it can get SOOO boring. I used never to study, but now, I have to study because the subjects have become really challenging. My advice, study if you get bad grades in a subject. If you really want, you can study for the subjects you're doing well in, but I suggest you study for the hard subjects first. • Damian

Studying is when you are applying your mind to either review work you have already learned or to learn and absorb new information. Although you are learning at school, studying is basically further careful observation of that subject. If you organize yourself well, you can include some study time into your afternoon/evening schedule. The amount of study time required depends on your school, and also what grades you want to achieve. Creating a study-friendly space in your home is also a good idea. • Josie

SUICIDE – Self-murder

I must admit, I've thought about suicide many times. I was massively depressed and just wanted it to end. People always say, "Think about the people you leave behind! How will they feel?" But no one ever thinks about how the suicidal person feels. If you think about suicide, tell somebody so you can get help to work through the situation that bothers you before it becomes totally desperate. • Damian

Suicide is a way to end it all; it is final – no second chance. It is very sad when a person reaches that stage. Depression sometimes comes before suicide. If you are depressed and are also having suicidal thoughts, please talk to somebody about it, or ask for help – you are a unique person who deserves to have a good life. There are always other choices, so do not think that the only choice is death. If you think a friend of yours is suicidal, talk to him or her about it, and tell an adult – maybe the help can save the person's life. • Josie

SUMMER CAMP – A place where students gather away from school for recreation

School camps are fun! You get to do a lot of fun stuff you normally wouldn't do and make new friends. Yes, I know, "Make new friends!" sounds really corny, but it's true – I've made friends at camps. If you don't like camps and are "forced" to go to one, try to see the positives. Camps are healthy for you, and you get some fresh air (listen to me, I'm a teenager and already talking like an adult ha-ha). I know … sounds sooo corny "get some fresh air," but seriously, when you're out in an area with nice fresh air, and you breathe it in, only then do you really appreciate and want fresh air. • Damian

For people with AS, camp can be a nightmare. It's a new place, new staff members, a whole lot of students in one area, new things happening each day, and so on. What we did for Damian's first summer camp was to tell him ahead of time what was going to happen each day; I made up a visual daily schedule. Also, we visited the campgrounds the week before so he could walk around, take photos and become familiar with it all. It was obviously very successful from what Damian has reported. • Josie

SWEARING – Cursing, using obscene language

Ha-ha-ha – swearing. I swear! I find swearing a good release of anger; when I hit my head, I swear! My parents let me swear, but if yours don't, I suggest you don't swear (at least not in front of them) because you'll get in trouble. • Damian

Well, yes, I allow my teenagers to swear – but not excessively and not in every situation! As Damian says, it serves as a form of small stress release, and it can be a form of expressing yourself. But if it is rude, repetitive, offensive or obsessive, then it becomes a problem. If you find that you can't stop yourself from blurting out swear words, you may need some help and use some strategies to teach your mind to stop your mouth from automatically saying the words. • Josie

TALENT – Gift, ability, expertise in a particular area or specific pursuit

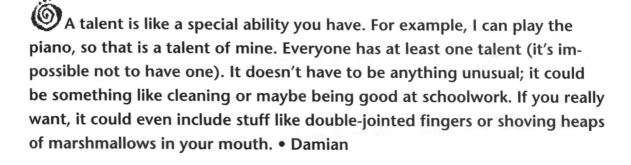A talent is like a special ability you have. For example, I can play the piano, so that is a talent of mine. Everyone has at least one talent (it's impossible not to have one). It doesn't have to be anything unusual; it could be something like cleaning or maybe being good at schoolwork. If you really want, it could even include stuff like double-jointed fingers or shoving heaps of marshmallows in your mouth. • Damian

Hmm, I can just see people discussing talents, "What's yours?" … "Oh, I can shove 20 marshmallows in my mouth" … joke. I know what Damian is trying to say: A talent is a special ability that you have. It can be silly or simple or so marvelously big that the whole world is amazed. My talent is writing and has been since I was a little girl. I now make a living from my talent; I am a full-time author of children and teenagers' books. What is your talent? If you aren't sure, ask a friend or family member; I bet they know! • Josie

TEACHERS – Persons who teach and instruct

Teachers are there to teach you, answer your questions and help you. If you're being bullied, you can tell a teacher. If you're confused, you can tell a teacher. If you get stressed, your teacher should be able to help you. If your teachers don't do these things, they are not doing their job. My teachers in elementary school were almost always reliable and almost always had something for me to do when I was stressed or needed help. They always explained things to me and helped me. You need to be able to talk to your teacher about these things. • Damian

⭐ Teachers have a pretty hard job nowadays. Class sizes are large, the curriculum changes frequently, and there are lots of students with special needs. A teacher is a guide, there to teach and guide you throughout your school years. Like everybody else, teachers have personalities too: Some are quiet, organized and disciplined; others are loud and chaotic. We noticed that Damian excelled under the guidance of male teachers. Some of the female teachers he had were a little too emotional for him, and often changed their moods, clothes and looks. This wasn't a good fit for Damian, who wanted consistency. The male teachers were more consistent and predictable in their behaviors and dress styles, and their expectations of classroom behavior were very clear. This is not necessarily a gender issue. Whenever possible, it is important to find a match between a student and his teacher's style. • Josie

TEARS – Drops of salty fluid secreted by the eyeball

🌀 Tears are a good thing. They are a physical expression of your emotions. If people say that you're a baby because you cry, they're stupid and have no right to judge you because they've either not been through anything you've experienced or they are hiding their emotions and are going to explode some day (not literally). I cry about five times a year, and when I say cry, I mean cry tears. Someone once laughed at me because he found out I used to cry at night before I went to sleep. I just ignored him. That guy was a typical example of someone who is very ignorant. • Damian

⭐ Tears are a result of some type of release. You can have happy tears or sad tears. Sometimes if you laugh very hard, your eyes might water, and you find that you are wiping away tears. But mainly tears are from crying if you are feeling sad. It is a good thing to express your feelings, not to suppress them. • Josie

TEENAGER – A boy or girl between the age of 13 to 19

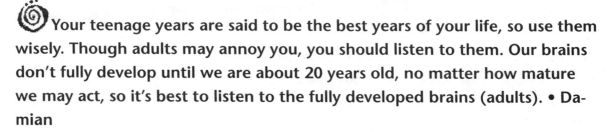

Your teenage years are said to be the best years of your life, so use them wisely. Though adults may annoy you, you should listen to them. Our brains don't fully develop until we are about 20 years old, no matter how mature we may act, so it's best to listen to the fully developed brains (adults). • Damian

Just remember that your parents were teenagers once! We have been through similar issues to what teens nowadays are going through. So if we come across as not being very understanding, it's because we are trying to save you from mistakes that we may have made. • Josie

TIME-AWAY – A period of time spent away from others

Time-away is a good way to wind down. When you're hyper or stressed and need to wind down, go to your room or some other safe place away from everything and everything and just relax. In my class in second grade, I used to have time-away area consisting of a beanbag chair and an egg timer that I would watch. It used to relax me. Try to find your own relaxation methods. That will become handy. • Damian

This is very similar to "quiet time." • Josie

TRUST – Reliance, confidence, dependence, belief and faith

Trust is one of the most important things in a relationship as a friend. I never tell anyone other people's secrets and that's why my friends trust me.

In eighth grade, a friend of mine betrayed my trust by blurting a secret of mine. As a result, I didn't trust him for two years. He hated it, so I made him earn my trust back, and now I trust him again. I know he won't tell others my secrets because he'd be too worried about losing my trust again (yet I still don't tell him everything just to be on the safe side). • Damian

Trust is a type of reliance on another person, in which you feel you can talk about anything without the other person judging you. It is when you feel totally safe to be who you are. To you, that may be your parents, a sibling, friend or a teacher. • Josie

TRUTH – Honest and frank statements

Truth is important. Never lie unless it's a white lie (lying so that you don't hurt someone's feelings). But sometimes the truth can hurt. For example, if you're in a relationship and someone tells you that your girlfriend is cheating on you, that hurts you emotionally. Although the truth can be bad, it is usually best to know it. • Damian

Honesty is the best option. Persons with AS are generally very honest people. If you are accused of not telling the truth, even if you are, it can be very frustrating and upsetting. If this happens to you, don't get angry, just keep telling the truth and speak to an adult. If it is an adult who doesn't believe you, tell another adult about it. • Josie

UNFAIR – Wrongful, unjust, biased and improper

Unfairness is common. Unfairness is when something is not equally shared, something happens that only benefits one person, someone gets punished for something they didn't do, or a "bad" person gets something "good." Even if it can sometimes seem that way, unfairness is <u>not</u> when you get a consequence because of an inappropriate action you performed. You will inevitably run into situations when you feel you are being unfairly treated, and sometimes you will just have to deal with it. Try to think of these events as temporary and believe that things will be fair eventually. If the unfairness benefits certain kids and you try to stop the unfairness, things could turn into verbal and physical bullying (see Bullying). This will only make things worse than they already are, and you will turn into the victim of the unfairness, so don't do it. • Damian

Unfairness is when you feel discriminated against or you are being judged incorrectly. It can be very frustrating if you think an issue is unfair. It is good to voice your opinion, but if your point of view is ignored, you may become even more frustrated. For example, in a football game, the referee may not have seen some foul play on the other side of the field, whereas half the crowd and the other players did. But because the referee didn't see it, he decides to ignore it. That seems very unfair to the person who was the victim of the foul play, and very unfair to the team if they lose because of it. But nothing can be done; the final word is that of the referee. This can happen in lots of different scenarios in life. Sometimes we just have to let go of our frustration and move on. If you truly believe something is unfair and you would like to do something about it, then follow the correct procedures, speak to an adult about it. If you feel you are being discriminated against, you have the right to be treated fairly, so speak up. • Josie

UNHAPPY – Sad, sorrowful, miserable and troubled

Unhappiness is an emotion that is the complete opposite of happiness. It is a state of negative emotions that makes you feel bad. Unhappiness is commonly expressed in sadness and depression (see Depression). This feeling is usually a way for your mind to tell you that something is wrong. It may be caused by a single incident, or it could be an outlook on your life. Many things can result in unhappiness, and it can be a big issue. If you're unhappy, acknowledge that it's your mind telling you that there is something wrong, try to find out what it is and then try to fix the problem. I do not recommend you avoid the problem, because it is just like running from it, and if you run from every problem in your life, you'll never achieve anything. Finding humor in a problem can be a great way to release stress (see Stress) as well as stop a problem from becoming an issue that will lead to unhappiness. • Damian

I think Damian's advice is great. If you try his strategies and still don't feel better, talk to a counselor or a doctor to see whether there's a chemical or physical reason behind your unhappiness. It could be due to a hormonal imbalance, or even due to food intolerances that affect your nervous system, and so on. • Josie

UNIVERSITY – Educational institution after senior high school

A university/college is an educational institution that provides post-high school courses. It's like a third level of school (elementary school, high school, and university), only it is not compulsory. It is required for certain jobs, such as being a doctor, dentist or an engineer. The way universities function is very different from high school. There is not nearly as much supervision and guidance, classes are not scheduled one right after the other, and so on, so a lot more responsibility is left up to you. Universities have their own cafeteria, dormitories (at least most) and shops, so it's like one big community. Another difference between high school and a university is that you specialize more in college. For example, if you wanted a job in science, you would study for a Bachelor of Science degree, specializing in science. If you choose a major (an area of interest to study) but later decide the courses are not right for you, you can change your major. If you find all this a bit overwhelming or scary to think about, you can go to an orientation day at a university. That's what I did, and it showed me so much about what happens at a university and made me look forward to going to a university even more than I already was. • Damian

You can also attend university on-line … like I am at the moment! • Josie

UNTIDY – Sloppy, disorderly, messy, not neat

Being untidy means that you are not very organized in putting away your things, in the way you dress, and so on. For example, I'm not very tidy in my room, because I do not like to put away my clothes. I just like to leave them on the floor. This makes me untidy. Though it is better to be a tidy person, sometimes you can be a little untidy. It's not like the world will explode if you are untidy. If someone else is being untidy, don't give a lecture on how he or she should be tidy, just ignore the untidiness; unless it directly affects you, it is none of your business. You decide your tidiness, and others decide theirs. • Damian

The downside about being untidy is that you never know where anything is. Damian's room has clean clothes and dirty clothes strewn across the floor. He walks over everything and then complains that his clean clothes smell dirty. If you want to be tidy, you could do what Damian's sister does: She has designated areas for things and lots of boxes and crates to put her stuff into. • Josie

VIOLENCE – Physical injury or damage as a result of fury or foul play

Violence can be emotional, verbal or physical. Violence is commonly used as a bullying (see Bullying) tool and can cause serious harm physically and mentally. Do not use any means of violence, except in self-defense. If someone wants to fight you, just say no and walk away. If this leads to insults, ignore them. If verbal violence is used against you (for example, an insult), it is also best to ignore it. Do not agree with the offender because that will just lead to more insults (I've seen people agree to get rid of the offender, and it doesn't work). (See Bullying to get a proper understanding on what to do when insulted.) Emotional violence is the aftermath of both verbal and physical violence. It's the damage done to the victim mentally. These effects can stay with the victim until he's an adult. • Damian

I heard a great saying the other day that I will share here: "Speak with your voice, not your fists." I think that it's a great way to sum up this entry on violence. • Josie

WANNABE – A person who wants to be like somebody else

Wannabes imitate and copy everything about the person they are imitating or what the type of person they are imitating does. Whatever you do, never be a wannabe; people can always tell when someone's a wannabe, and the wannabe will either be bullied (see Bullying) or disliked by other students (see also Peer Pressure). • Damian

Yes, it is best to be yourself. "Wannabe" is a combination word made up of the words "want to be." It's strange because teens love to be independent, and yet they follow other groups and want to fit in and be like others; it's very confusing. I think people with AS don't have to worry about being wannabes; you are pretty unique. But if you are trying to socially fit in and have chosen somebody you would like to be similar to – that's okay, just be inspired by them to create your own style, don't follow them around constantly and copy them. • Josie

X-PLANATION – The act of interpreting or clarifying

I know the word explanation doesn't start with an X, and I told mom, but she said she didn't have anything for X and that we needed a word to complete the alphabet. An explanation means informing somebody about something. For example, if someone named "One" asks another person named "Two" what a chair is, "Two" would explain by saying that it is a four-legged object that is used to sit on. Explanations usually answer questions that involve a "why"; for example, "One" asks "Two" why a dog scratches itself. "Two" would then explain by telling "One" that the dog has fleas. You should never be restricted from an explanation. If you want one, ask, especially if the person you're asking is a teacher. • Damian

 Yes, sorry for the misspelling, but we really needed something for X! • Josie

YOU – Yourself, thee, thou, you alone!

You are you. What else can I say? • Damian

YOU are a very unique individual, and nobody else is like you, so celebrate this fact. • Josie

Z

ZITS – Pimples and blemishes

Zits are pimples that are red and sometimes white. They usually come up on your face and are a result of several things. Either you are under stress or you ate something that your body doesn't like (but usually tastes good, like chocolate). If you get pimples, don't panic; just put some pimple cream on or don't do anything. Other students get pimples as well, and the only time people mention and look at your pimples is usually when they are whiteheads. People don't like looking at white pimples, and they might tease you about it. But if it is just a normal red pimple, don't worry about it and pretend it isn't there. No one will care, and neither should you. Oh, and also, if you find pimples on your back or shoulder or somewhere, don't panic! It's normal for teenagers. It's due to hormones and stuff (see also Acne). • Damian

Yes, pimples are caused by hormonal changes, extra testosterone, and also can be caused by dietary factors; for example, too much sugar in your diet. Damian just recently (after he wrote his piece above) had a problem with pimples, so he made a decision (after his sister and I told him about it a thousand times) to stop drinking soft drinks each day. He started drinking lots of water instead; it has made such a difference to his face – fewer pimples! • Josie

Faded Hope

Damian Santomauro

"What's the problem, doctor?" the father begins to ask
"Will raising him be such a difficult task?"

The answer to that question provokes fear and denial
For training to be normal could take a while

And when the child attends his first day at school
All the students are horribly cruel

Each and every abuse adds a layer of stress
All stored inside like a horrible mess

But when the child is full, it is all too much to hold in
So he throws his stress to the world like a bin

When this happens too often, the expression changes its way
Now released stronger but slower, and darkness has its say

Now instead of receiving, the child sends out fear
Repaying the students for the shedding of the child's tear

Finally at high school, the students accept the child
For the child has changed and the bullying is mild

Then the child sees the same bullying as before
In someone who is receiving the same treatment he had before

Now that the child has a normal life with all the abuse run dry
He is still haunted by his memories, which would make the average person cry

Absent Tolerance

Damian Santomauro

I see a special girl
Crying about something unknown
If she wanted, she could look as a pearl
But others think otherwise, as they have shown

And as I see my friends
Snigger and laugh
My subconscious sends
Memories, which make me barf

But when I get upset
My friends don't know why
Because it's the side of me they've never met
Which is hidden by a lie

Why don't people understand?
And be tolerant and kind?
It isn't too much to demand!
Do you think they'd really mind?

If only they'd appreciate
What it's like to be happy
To not be enraged by hate
Or be treated like they need a nappy

If only they knew
The secret and explore
If only they'd like to do
Something a little bit more ...

ALPHABETICAL LIST OF TOPICS

ABUSE 1

ACNE 1

ADOLESCENCE 2

ADULTHOOD 2

ADVICE 3

ALCOHOL 4

ANGER 4

ANXIETY 5

APOLOGY 6

ARGUMENTS 7

ASPERGER SYNDROME 8

BELIEVING IN YOURSELF 8

BITING 9

BODY SHAPE 10

BULLYING 11

CAREER 12

CHAT ROOMS 13

COMEBACK 14

COMMUNICATION 14

CONFIDENCE 15

CONFUSION 16

COOL 17

COUNSELOR 18

CRIME 18

DAD 19

DATING 20

DECISIONS 20

DEPRESSION 21

DIAGNOSIS 22

DIET 23

DISABILITY 23

DIVORCE 24

DOCTOR 25

DRUGS 25

ECCENTRIC/ODD 26

EMBARRASSING MOMENTS 26

EMOTIONS...................................... 27

EMPATHY 28

ENEMIES.. 29

EXAMS 29

EXERCISE 30

EYE CONTACT 30

FAMILY 31

FASHION 32

FEAR 33

FIGHT 33

FORGIVENESS.................................. 34

FRIENDSHIP 35

FUN... 37

GOALS... 38

GOSSIP.. 38

GUILT 39

HARASSMENT.................................. 40

HATE 40

HEALTH 41

HEARTBREAK 41

HELP 42

HOBBY 42

HOMEWORK 43

HOMOSEXUAL 43

HORMONES 44

HYGIENE............................... 44

INDEPENDENCE 45

INSULT 46

INTELLIGENT 46

INTERNET 47

JEALOUSY 48

JOB 48

JOKES 49

JOURNAL 50

KINDNESS 51

KISSING................................ 52

LAZY 52

LIE 53

LONELY 54

LOVE 55

MANNERS 56

MEDIATION........................... 57

MEDITATION 57

METAPHOR............................ 57

MISTAKE 58

MOBILE PHONE...................... 59

MOM 59

MONEY 60

MORALS 60

MUSIC.................................. 61

NAME-CALLING 62

NORMAL 62

OBSESSIONS 63

ODORS.................................. 64

ORGANIZED 64

OUTCAST 65

PARENTS............................... 66

PARTIES 66

PEERS 67

PERSONAL SAFETY................... 68

POLICE 68

POPULARITY 69

PROBLEM-SOLVING.................. 70

PUNISHMENT......................... 70

QUESTION 70

QUIET TIME 71

REBELLIOUS 72

RELATIVES 73

RELAXATION........................... 73

RESPONSIBLE.......................... 74

REVENGE 74

RULES 75

RUMOR 75

RUNAWAY 76

SAD 77

SARCASM 77

SCHOOL................................ 78

SELF-ESTEEM 79

SECRETS 80

SENSORY OVERLOAD 80

SHADOWING 81

SHAVING 82

SIBLING 82

SLEEPLESS 83

SLEEPOVER 84

SOCIALIZING 84

SOCIAL OCCASIONS 85

SOCIAL SKILLS 86

SPECIAL EDUCATION 87

STALKING 87

STRATEGIES 88

STRESS 88

STUDY 89

SUICIDE 90

SUMMER CAMP 90

SWEARING 91

TALENT 92

TEACHERS 92

TEARS 93

TEENAGER 94

TIME-AWAY 94

TRUST 94

TRUTH 95

UNFAIR 96

UNHAPPY 97

UNIVERSITY 97

UNTIDY 98

VIOLENCE 99

WANNABE 99

X-PLANATION 100

YOU 100

ZITS 101

ALPHABETICAL LIST OF TOPICS BY CATEGORY

BEHAVIORS
BEHAVIOR
BITING
ECCENTRIC/ODD
EYE CONTACT
LAZY
LIE
MANNERS
MORALS
OBSESSIONS
SLEEPLESS
TRUST
UNTIDY

BULLYING
ABUSE
BULLYING
ENEMIES
GOSSIP
HARASSMENT
INSULT
NAME-CALLING
OUTCAST
RUMOR
SARCASM
SHADOWING

COMMUNICATION
APOLOGY
CHAT ROOMS
COMMUNICATION

CONFUSION
INTERNET
METAPHOR
MOBILE PHONE
SECRETS
TRUTH

DIAGNOSIS
ADULTHOOD
ASPERGER SYNDROME
DIAGNOSIS
DISABILITY

CONSEQUENCES
ALCOHOL
ARGUMENTS
CRIME
DRUGS
FIGHT
POLICE
PUNISHMENT
REBELLIOUS
RESPONSIBLE
REVENGE
RULES
RUNAWAY
STALKING
SWEARING
VIOLENCE

EMOTIONS
ANGER
ANXIETY
DEPRESSION
EMBARRASSING MOMENTS
EMOTIONS
EMPATHY
FEAR
FORGIVENESS
GUILT
HATE
HEARTBREAK
JEALOUSY
JOURNAL
LONELY
LOVE
SAD
STRESS
SUICIDE
TEARS
UNHAPPY

FAMILY
DAD
DIVORCE
FAMILY
MOM
PARENTS
RELATIVES
SIBLING

FRIENDSHIP
FRIENDSHIP
JOKES
KINDNESS

PHYSICAL/
WELL-BEING
ACNE
BODY SHAPE
DIET
DOCTOR
EXERCISE
HEALTH
HOBBY
HOMOSEXUAL
HORMONES
HYGIENE
MEDITATION
ODORS
PERSONAL SAFETY
RELAXATION
SHAVING
ZITS

SCHOOL
CAREER
EXAMS
HOMEWORK
PEERS
SCHOOL
SPECIAL EDUCATION
STUDY
TEACHERS
UNIVERSITY

SELF-ESTEEM
BELIEVING IN YOURSELF
CONFIDENCE
INDEPENDENCE
INTELLIGENT
NORMAL
SELF-ESTEEM
TALENT
YOU

SOCIALIZING
ADOLESCENCE
COOL
DATING
FASHION
FUN
KISSING
PARTIES
POPULARITY
SLEEPOVER
SOCIALIZING
SOCIAL OCCASIONS
SOCIAL SKILLS
SUMMER CAMP
TEENAGER
WANNABE

STRATEGIES
ADVICE
COMEBACK
COUNSELOR
DECISIONS
GOALS
HELP
JOB

MEDIATION
MISTAKE
MONEY
MUSIC
ORGANIZED
PROBLEM-SOLVING
QUESTION
QUIET TIME
SENSORY OVERLOAD
STRATEGIES
TIME-AWAY
UNFAIR
X-PLANATION

Note: The dictionary terms came from *Webster's New World Dictionary & Thesaurus* CD.

AAPC

Autism Asperger Publishing Co.
P.O. Box 23173
Shawnee Mission, Kansas 66283-0173
www.asperger.net